DEFUSING OPPOSITIONAL DEFIANT DISORDER

7 SIMPLE STRATEGIES TO FOSTER A RESILIENT
PARENT-CHILD CONNECTION

ROSE LYONS

CONTENTS

Prepare to embark on an emotional rollercoaster as we delve deep into the world of Oppositional Defiant Disorder (ODD). This book isn't just about facts; it's about tapping into your heart and soul to understand the challenges, triumphs, and transformations that lie ahead. Get ready to gain a unique perspective on your child's journey, their struggles, and the incredible potential for growth. In this unique journey towards understanding and managing ODD, you're encouraged to have a notepad handy, as there are interactive elements that invite you to reflect, answer questions, and embark on a personal exploration of this complex condition.

In addition to this, a companion guide is available for a more comprehensive experience. The 'Defusing Oppositional Defiant Disorder Workbook' offers bonus materials that complement this book. Inside, you'll find additional information on behavioral contracts, rewards, consequences, daily gratitude practices, and exercises specifically designed for parents and children to strengthen their bond. Either way, be sure to have something available, as the reflection sections are key to ensure that the you get the most from the book and the information is solidified.

So whether you dive into the interactive elements within these pages or opt for the companion guide, you're on a path towards deeper understanding, improved communication, and a more harmonious life for you and your child. Let's get started!

FREE BONUS CHAPTER

By adding this bonus chapter to your collection, you'll have an invaluable resource to complement the main book. It's an opportunity to dive deeper into the subject, gain more insights, and empower yourself with even more solutions.

Don't miss out on this exciting addition to your reading experience. Get your FREE bonus chapter today and unlock a wealth of knowledge to support your journey.

INTRODUCTION

If you want something you have never had, you must be willing to do something you have never done.

— THOMAS JEFFERSON

Imagine a moment that prompted you to seek answers, a turning point when you knew there had to be a better way. It's not just the title of this book that brought you here; it's the desire for change, the quest for a harmonious life with your child who's challenged by Oppositional Defiant Disorder (ODD). I understand where you are in your journey, the frustrations, and the longing for solutions.

Raising a child with ODD is distinct from raising a neurotypical child, and it requires tailored approaches that address the specific needs and dynamics of this condition. While some might not fully comprehend the nuances of your situation, the strategies presented here are rooted in practicality and aimed at equipping both you and your child with the skills needed to navigate these complex waters. This isn't about sentimentality; it's about providing genuine hope and fostering lifelong skills for your child's well-being and growth.

However, it's important to recognize that not everyone will agree with the approaches discussed in this book. Some family members or other parents might view these strategies as letting the child off too easily. In such situations, it's crucial to remember that you are the one actively seeking education and guidance through this book. You are the parent facing the unique challenges of raising a child with ODD.

As you delve into this book, envision a life where daily conflicts are replaced with understanding, defiance transforms into cooperation, and your relationship with your child flourishes. Picture a harmonious household where your child manages their behaviors and thrives emotionally and socially. Visualize a future where you, as a parent, feel confident and empowered in your ability to nurture your child's growth and well-being.

For the last 15 years, my unwavering commitment has been to delve deep into the intricacies of parenting children who are neurodivergent, including those grappling with Oppositional Defiant Disorder.

Together, let's embark on a journey of discovery and transformation, guided by the knowledge and experiences shared within these pages.

LIFETIME PREVALENCE OF ODD

ODD is a prevalent mental health issue that affects numerous individuals. The National Comorbidity Survey Replication performed research that disclosed within the examined population, 10.2% of grown-ups had faced ODD at a certain juncture. The results indicated that 11% of men and 9% of women were affected by ODD (Waldman, 2022). This study underscores the importance of early intervention and management of ODD symptoms to prevent long-lasting adverse outcomes.

LONG-TERM EFFECTS OF UNMANAGED ODD

When ODD remains unaddressed, it can lead to significant life challenges and serious antisocial behavior in adulthood. Untreated children with ODD may face difficulties forming social connections, academic achievements, and job opportunities as they grow. Moreover, ODD often coincides with other mental health issues like depression, anxiety, and substance addiction, intensifying negative consequences (Raypole & Gotter, 2021).

This book introduces a new parenting perspective that not only restores harmony to your home but also guides your child toward a more promising future, equipping them with vital coping skills and fostering cherished family memories.

I understand each family's journey is unique. That's why I'll share three diverse case studies of children with ODD, aged 5 to 18, for you to learn from. I also want to acknowledge what led you to this book. Whether it was a difficult day with your child or realizing your current strategies aren't working, know that you are not alone. This book will provide the guidance needed for genuine progress.

Throughout this book, I'll incorporate interactive components and reflection segments at the end of each chapter to reinforce your understanding and strategize your future actions. Drawing from my in-depth knowledge, I'll offer medical clarifications and trigger alerts whenever appropriate.

Upon completing this book, you will gain invaluable insight into ODD, effective methods for guiding your child's behavior, and the resources to help them thrive. While it took me years to acquire this wisdom, it's truly rewarding to share this information so that you can experience a more joyful bond with your child and a peaceful home. If you are prepared to embark on the journey toward a better family life, let's start together.

1

UNDERSTANDING ODD

The greatest pleasure in life is doing what people say you cannot do.

— WALTER BAGEHOT

Have you ever encountered a child who continually questioned rules, challenged authority, and seemed to thrive on defiance? These actions might not be just a phase. We delve into the world of ODD in this chapter, learning about its warning signs, symptoms, and essential information. Understanding the fundamentals of ODD can help you better prepare yourself to support and nurture your child, fostering a future filled with happiness and health.

WHAT IS ODD?

A pattern of continuous anger, irritability, argumentativeness, or defiance toward authority figures is the hallmark of ODD, a behavioral condition. Children with ODD frequently struggle to control their emotions and become easily irritated, angry, and spiteful. If addressed, ODD symptoms can last into adolescence and adulthood and typically start in childhood.

Some typical signs of ODD include:

1. Frequent fits of rage
2. Arguing excessively with grown-ups
3. Refusing to adhere to instructions or rules
4. Consciously aiming to irritate or anger other people
5. Accusing people of your errors or bad actions
6. Being sensitive, easily irritated, or angry
7. Being vindictive or seeking retribution (*Oppositional defiant disorder*, 2023).

It's important to acknowledge that parents of children with ODD may face challenges enforcing rules and managing their behavior. For those with teenagers, the road may look a little different as they are older and require more attention to modifying the underlying reasons behind their behavior. However, practical strategies can help navigate these difficulties, including setting clear boundaries and consequences, focusing on positive behaviors, and using positive reinforcement to encourage desired conduct.

AT WHAT AGE IS ODD MOST OFTEN DIAGNOSED?

While signs of Oppositional Defiant Disorder (ODD) can manifest as early as age three, it is typically diagnosed in children around the age of eight. ODD tends to affect boys more often than girls and frequently co-occurs with other mental health conditions, such as Attention Deficit Hyperactivity Disorder (ADHD). If left untreated, ODD can persist for many years, extending into adulthood, significantly hampering social, cognitive, and occupational functioning.

The CDC underscores the critical importance of early diagnosis and intervention in shaping a child's future outcomes when addressing behavioral disorders. For parents or caregivers who harbor concerns about ODD or other behavioral challenges in their children, it is essential to proactively seek professional guidance. A thorough assessment performed by a qualified mental health specialist is indispensable for obtaining an accurate diagnosis and devising an efficacious treatment strategy (What is Children's, 2023).

It is crucial to acknowledge that, although ODD presents significant challenges, resources and assistance are readily accessible to aid parents and children alike. Effectively managing ODD behaviors and helping the child achieve their full potential can be greatly facilitated by seeking guidance from mental health professionals, educators, as well as connecting with other parents who have experienced similar situations.

THE ROLE OF GENETICS AND ENVIRONMENT IN ODD DEVELOPMENT

Delving into the factors contributing to ODD's development is vital for devising efficient support systems and interventions. It is crucial to explore the relationship between genetic and environmental aspects, as they jointly shape the emergence of ODD in children.

Investigations have shown that genetic factors play a considerable part in ODD occurrence. Research involving twins and family members demonstrates that the disorder often appears in families, with siblings of affected children having a greater chance of exhibiting ODD symptoms (Faraone & Larsson, 2019). Furthermore, specific gene variants have been connected to an elevated risk of developing ODD. This genetic susceptibility implies that some children might be more prone to the disorder due to hereditary characteristics.

Nonetheless, it's essential not to downplay the influence of environmental factors in developing ODD. A child's upbringing, life experiences, and surroundings significantly impact their mental health and behavior. Various environmental factors have been recognized as contributing to ODD onset.

- **Parenting approaches**: Inconsistent discipline, excessively strict or permissive parenting, and absence of positive reinforcement may contribute to ODD development. Children might react to these methods with resistance and defiance, perpetuating a cycle of adverse behavior.
- **Family dynamics**: Elevated levels of family strife, parental substance abuse, or mental health problems can generate a stressful atmosphere for a child, potentially intensifying ODD symptoms.
- **Traumatic events**: Encountering trauma, abuse, or neglect can profoundly affect a child's mental health and potentially provoke the onset of ODD.
- **Socioeconomic elements**: Lower socioeconomic status has been linked with a higher occurrence of ODD, with financial strain and restricted access to resources possibly contributing to the development of the disorder.
- **Peer relationships**: Struggles establishing and maintaining healthy peer connections can lead to social isolation and may exacerbate ODD symptoms.

The interplay between genetics and environmental factors is intricate, and determining each aspect's precise role in ODD development isn't always straightforward. A blend of genetic predisposition and environmental influences likely contributes to the appearance of the disorder in each distinct case.

Understanding this intricate relationship is paramount for developing effective intervention strategies for children with ODD. Early identification of risk factors and targeted support can play a pivotal role in preventing the disorder from taking root or worsening. Parenting interventions that emphasize positive communication, consistent discipline, and a nurturing environment can counterbalance genetic predispositions and the impact of environmental stressors.

Moreover, addressing environmental factors such as family discord, trauma, and financial stress is essential in minimizing their influence on a child's mental well-being. Ensuring access to appropriate mental health services, family therapy, and social support can significantly assist children with ODD and their families in overcoming these challenges.

In summary, the emergence of ODD involves a complex interplay of genetic and environmental factors. Recognizing and addressing these elements is critical for providing support to children with ODD and their families.

Armed with a thorough grasp of the disorder's underlying causes, parents, educators, and healthcare practitioners can join forces to foster a nurturing and reassuring atmosphere for children predisposed to ODD, promoting improved outcomes for everyone concerned.

HOW ODD CAN CAUSE FURTHER KNOCK-ON REACTIONS

ODD's impact reaches beyond the child, touching their family, peers, and the broader community. Kids with ODD frequently encounter numerous obstacles, such as diminished academic progress, tense connections with family and friends, heightened susceptibility to mental health struggles like depression and anxiety, and a sense of loneliness. Various factors, such as the nurturing environment in which the child is raised, their social support network, and the financial resources available, whether from parents, schools, or the community, can potentially impact the severity of these outcomes.

Typically, it is an absolute necessity to wrap your head around the fact that while some sort of oppositional behavior is indeed a customary aspect of children's development, frequent and sustained hostility and obstinacy can turn into a problematic predicament when it messes with the child's academic, social, and familial life. Specifically, children grappling with ODD could find themselves caught in a whirlwind of disruption in class, bickering with instructors, and adamantly refusing to conform to rules and regulations. Alas, maintaining positive relationships with friends, family, and authority figures might challenge them, as their irritable and hostile demeanor could lead to strained connections.

Similarly, it's important to highlight that children with ODD are more likely to develop various mental health conditions, including depression, anxiety, and substance abuse, both during their youth and as they transition into adulthood. In severe cases, the defiant conduct of children with ODD may also bring about felony problems of vandalism, theft, and bodily aggression. They can also emerge as socially remote because of their conduct, mainly due to emotions of loneliness and rejection.

It is crucial to remember that with early identification and intervention, children with ODD can examine coping abilities to control their conduct, enhance their relationships with others, and prevail academically and socially.

MAIN SIGNS AND SYMPTOMS OF ODD ACCORDING TO THE DSM

The Diagnostic and Statistical Manual of Mental Disorders (DSM) is an American Psychiatric Association guide that lists installed standards for analyzing some intellectual disorders, including ODD.

According to the DSM-5, the primary standards for the analysis of ODD are listed below.

1. **Consistent sample of poor conduct**: Children with ODD show a continual sample of defiant, hostile, and poor conduct closer to authority figures,

including parents, teachers, and different adults. This conduct isn't simply occasional, however. Instead, it occurs regularly and is constant over time.

2. **Intensity of behavior**: The negative actions of children with ODD are often more severe and excessive compared to those of a typically uncooperative child. They may frequently experience tantrums, engage in spiteful behavior, and purposefully attempt to upset or disappoint others.

3. **Obstacles in daily living**: Kids with ODD can encounter hardships in different areas, including education, family life, and social situations. Their behavior can significantly impact their daily functioning and relationships.

4. **Duration of symptoms**: For an analysis of ODD, the poor conduct must have endured for (as a minimum) six months (*DSM-5 child*, n.d.).

ODD and various mental health conditions are regularly identified, including ADHD, depression, tension disorders, and post-traumatic stress disorder (PTSD). Research proposes that as many as 60% of children with ODD may also have ADHD, and as many as 40% can also have a temper or tension disorder (Connor & Doerfler, 2008).

Inattention, impulsivity, and hyperactivity are some of the symptoms of ADHD. The behavioral and social challenges children with ADHD frequently face overlap with those of

ODD. For instance, ODD and ADHD can lead to disruptive behavior at home and in the classroom since both conditions make it difficult to obey rules.

Together with ODD, depression and anxiety disorders are frequently identified. Children with ODD may struggle to control their moods and feel overpowered by their strong emotions. ODD symptoms may emerge similar to how anxiety problems can make a child feel stressed, anxious, or overwhelmed. Lastly, ODD symptoms may be more likely to appear in children who have encountered traumatic situations, and PTSD is also a frequently identified comorbid disorder.

In diagnosing and addressing ODD, it's essential to consider other conditions. A thorough assessment can help identify any underlying issues causing the child's symptoms. This method could result in more efficient and customized support, concentrating on particular areas of the child's needs, including their intellectual, social, and emotional development.

Moreover, untreated ODD can progress into a more severe behavioral disorder. This escalated condition, known as conduct disorder, is marked by extreme defiance of rules, aggressive behaviors towards others, and, in some cases, involvement in criminal activities. Therefore, early intervention to address ODD symptoms is crucial in preventing the development of more serious issues.

Finally, ODD is usually diagnosed with other mental health issues such as ADHD, depression, anxiety disorders, and PTSD. A thorough evaluation is required to find any coexisting disorders that might be causing the child's symptoms. Taking care of these underlying difficulties can help the child operate more generally and help stop the emergence of more serious concerns.

REFLECTION SECTION

After delving into the chapter on Oppositional Defiant Disorder (ODD), consider the following prompts to deepen your understanding and apply the insights:

Recognizing Behaviors: Take a moment to note specific behaviors you've observed in your child that may align with ODD tendencies.

Discipline Challenges: Reflect on the challenges you've encountered when disciplining your child. What strategies have you tried, and what has been effective or challenging?

Impact on School and Social Life: Explore how your child's behavior has affected their school performance and interactions with peers. Are there patterns that need attention?

New Techniques: Identify the fresh techniques you've gleaned from this chapter. How do you envision implementing these strategies to manage your child's behavior?

Anticipating Challenges: Consider potential challenges as you integrate these new tactics. What obstacles might arise, and how can you proactively address them?

Seeking Support: Reflect on any additional help or resources you might require to navigate these challenges successfully. Are there areas where you need guidance or expertise?

Action Plan: Outline how to apply these new tactics in daily interactions with your child. How will you address their conduct effectively in the upcoming weeks?

Remember, the purpose of these reflections is to aid you in digesting what you've learned, pinpointing areas where you could benefit from extra assistance, and devising a plan to implement these newfound strategies. Your commitment to these insights can impact your child's journey toward positive behavior and healthy relationships.

After delving into the chapter on ODD, let's take a moment to self-reflect as parents. Consider the following prompts:

1. What behaviors have you seen in your child that might point to ODD?
2. What difficulties have you had so far with disciplining your child?
3. How has your child's behavior affected their schoolwork and interactions with other children?

4. What fresh techniques have you learned from this chapter that might be useful in controlling your child's behavior?
5. What challenges do you foresee when you put these new tactics into practice?
6. What additional help or resources would you need to manage your child's behavior effectively?
7. How will you start implementing these new tactics and dealing with your child's conduct in the coming weeks?

Remember that the goal of reflecting is to aid parents in processing what they have learned, identifying areas where they require additional support, and developing a strategy for implementing new tactics.

STORY

In a small suburban home, Emily and her son, Ethan, shared their daily lives. From the very beginning, Ethan's boundless energy set him apart. Yet, as he continued to grow, Emily couldn't help but notice the peculiar nature of his behavior. At just two years old, he exhibited frequent temper tantrums that seemed to arise out of thin air, leaving Emily puzzled and increasingly concerned.

As time passed, Ethan's defiance became more pronounced. Simple tasks often led to arguments as he refused to follow his mother's requests. While well-meaning friends and family dismissed it as a phase, Emily's intuition told her something deeper was at play.

Countless parents are trapped in a swirling vortex of bewilderment and desolation, feeling utterly adrift and powerless. You may be experiencing a whirlwind of emotions as you strive to offer your child the necessary assistance and direction to find their way in life. In the following chapter, we'll explore the intricate aspects of this condition and discuss the internal dynamics of children with ODD.

SELF-ANALYSIS QUESTIONNAIRE FOR PARENTS MANAGING A DEFIANT CHILD

Please respond to the following questions to the best of your information and abilities. This questionnaire will assist you in determining whether the conduct of your child may be exhibiting ODD. Please respond as sincerely as possible; there is no right or wrong response.

Choose from:
Infrequently, Sometimes, Often, All the time

1. Does your child regularly argue with parents or other adults, such as teachers?
2. Does your child object when you ask them to do something or when you make rules for them?
3. Does your child purposefully irritate or bother other people, like their siblings or friends, a lot?

4. Does your child shift blame to others and refuse to accept responsibility for their mistakes or misbehavior?
5. Does your child refuse to comply with requests or tasks, even age-appropriate?
6. Do you often notice that your child is angry or bitter?
7. Does your child frequently seek retribution or harbor resentment?
8. Is your child frequently spiteful or vengeful?
9. Has your child's behavior seriously hampered their ability to function or maintain relationships on a day-to-day basis?
10. Has your child exhibited unfavorable behavior for at least a year?

Scoring:

If you have chosen "Often" or "All the Time" for four or more items, it's advisable to consult a mental health professional for a thorough assessment. Please note that this questionnaire does not offer a diagnosis; a professional assessment is crucial for an accurate diagnosis and appropriate treatment plan.

Note: The purpose of this questionnaire is not to be a substitute for expert therapeutic guidance, examination, or care. If you have any concerns about a medical problem, consult your doctor or another skilled healthcare professional.

IS THERE A NEUROLOGICAL BASIS FOR THE PROBLEM?

There may be a neurological basis for ODD, according to research. Compared with children typically developing, children with ODD have been discovered to have different brain structures and functions. Particularly, they have diminished activity in brain parts connected to impulse control, emotional management, and social cognition (Matthys et al., 2012).

A study discovered that children with ODD had lower prefrontal brain activity, which is in charge of executive abilities like planning, drive control, and decision-making (*Frequently Asked Questions*, n.d.). Anterior cingulate mind activity, which is important for emotional control and understanding, was lower in ODD children, in accordance with another study (Noordermeer et al., 2016).

2

INSIDE AN ODD MIND

Everything we do, every thought we've ever had, is produced by the human brain. But exactly how it operates remains one of the biggest mysteries, and the more we probe its secrets, the more surprises we find.

— NEIL DEGRASSE TYSON

A s caregivers of children with ODD, it may be challenging to understand the basic parts of their minds. But what if we step inside their world and see stuff from their perspective? What would we find? Would it change the way we approach and support them? Within the chapter, we'll investigate the unique and often misinterpreted perspective of the different minds and gain insights into how we can better connect with and help our loved ones with this condition.

WHAT ARE THE MAIN RISK FACTORS FOR ODD?

Many elements play a role in the emergence of ODD, a childhood behavioral issue marked by enduring resistance, noncompliance, and antagonism toward those in authority. Genetic influences may play a significant role, with children with a family history of ODD or related behavioral disorders more likely to experience the condition. Though not all children who experience adverse circumstances will develop ODD, these factors can contribute to the formation of maladaptive coping mechanisms, such as disruptive behaviors characteristic of ODD.

Parenting style plays a pivotal role in the development of ODD. Harsh, inconsistent, or neglectful parenting practices elevate the risk of ODD, whereas positive, nurturing, and consistent parenting approaches can mitigate this risk and enhance outcomes for children grappling with this condition. Establishing clear rules, applying praise, providing support, and active engagement in a child's life are linked to decreased ODD symptoms. Conversely, harsh disciplinary methods, shouting, and critical behavior are associated with heightened symptoms of ODD.

ADHD and other related conditions frequently have shared underlying risk factors and might impact the manifestation of ODD. For instance, a child with ADHD could exhibit impulsive and hyperactive behaviors that resemble those found in ODD. In contrast, a child with anxiety or depression might demonstrate avoidance behaviors or emotional instability, resulting in defiant and oppositional conduct. Addressing and treating these co-occurring conditions alongside ODD is vital to improving overall outcomes.

WHAT CAN BE DONE?

One methodology is to zero in on further developing the nurturing style and climate in which the child is raised. Investigations have discovered that certain nurturing practices, like encouraging feedback, clear assumptions, and steady outcomes, can be compelling in diminishing oppositional and defiant behaviors in children with ODD. Mastering regulating our emotions before addressing our child's outbursts is fundamental in aligning our actions with our words. Fostering a meaningful relationship with your child goes beyond mere authoritative directives. After all, how can we expect them to navigate their emotions if we're merely dictating their feelings and responses?

Another approach involves medication providing neurobiological support. Prescription stimulants, mood stabilizers, and antidepressants have been employed to address ODD symptoms, particularly in cases where comorbidity with

ADHD or other conditions exists. However, it's important to view medication as just one facet of a comprehensive treatment strategy, encompassing behavioral interventions and therapy.

Cognitive-behavioral therapy (CBT) and dialectical behavior therapy (DBT) are often used to show adaptive, social, and fundamental abilities to people with ODD. These therapies can assist people with figuring out how to manage their feelings, further developing relational abilities, and fostering critical thinking components. CBT and DBT have been demonstrated to be successful in decreasing oppositional and defiant behaviors in children and adolescents with ODD.

THE ROLE OF TECHNOLOGY AND ODD

The impact of technology on today's world is continuously growing, and its effects on individuals diagnosed with ODD are no different. As digital tools and resources multiply, technology holds the power to reshape how ODD is approached, treated, and comprehended.

One remarkable aspect of technology's influence is the increasing presence of telehealth services. For children with ODD and their families, telehealth can be a priceless asset. It provides greater access to mental health experts specializing in ODD, particularly those in rural or distant locations. Furthermore, telehealth platforms allow families to participate in therapy sessions within the familiarity of their homes, minimizing the stress and unease associated with in-person appointments.

Another significant advancement is the emergence of online support communities. These spaces offer a secure environment for parents, caregivers, and individuals with ODD to share their journeys, exchange recommendations, and form bonds with others who comprehend their difficulties. The sense of unity fostered by these virtual networks can be key in reducing feelings of loneliness and fostering resilience.

Besides telehealth and online support communities, technology has spawned a range of digital tools designed to assist in treating and managing ODD. Mobile apps and websites present resources such as behavioral monitoring, tailored coping techniques, and educational content to help individuals with ODD and their caregivers better grasp and tackle the disorder. These tools can be particularly helpful for observing progress, pinpointing triggers, and supporting therapy objectives.

Moreover, technology has played a crucial role in propelling the research and understanding of ODD. Gathering and analyzing data from various digital sources–including online questionnaires, wearable devices, and electronic health records–has enabled the recognition of patterns and tendencies that can guide future treatment methods.

While technology presents numerous advantages for individuals with ODD and their families, it is vital to recognize the possible drawbacks. For instance, excessive use of screen-based devices has been connected to heightened irritability, sleep disruption, and diminished attention spans—factors that can intensify ODD symptoms. Thus, balancing using technology's benefits and mitigating its adverse effects is vital for achieving optimal results.

To sum up, the role of technology concerning ODD is diverse. It presents tremendous potential for revolutionizing how the disorder is handled and treated. Telehealth services, online support communities, digital tools, and data-driven research all create more effective, accessible, and individualized approaches to ODD care. By capitalizing on technology's potential while staying aware of its limitations, a more promising future lies ahead for those affected by ODD and their families.

WHAT HAPPENS IN THE BRAIN OF AN ODD CHILD?

Oppositional Defiant Disorder (ODD) is a neurodevelopmental condition that affects a child's ability to manage their emotions, behavior, and thoughts. It's essential to grasp that the challenging behaviors exhibited by children with ODD are not the result of deliberate misbehavior or a lack of discipline. Instead, they stem from underlying biological factors.

A significant aspect of ODD revolves around the brain's reward system, particularly the dopamine pathway, which is responsible for feelings of pleasure and reward. In children with ODD, this system often malfunctions, causing them to have an increased aversion to rewards. Consequently, they may impulsively seek gratification, sometimes aggressively, making it challenging to control their actions and make appropriate decisions.

Research has shown that children with ODD tend to exhibit reduced activity in the prefrontal cortex, a part of the brain responsible for self-regulation and decision-making. This reduced activity can make managing their behavior and responding appropriately in social situations difficult.

While ODD is a complex condition, there are treatments that can effectively support children with this disorder. In some cases, medications such as stimulants and antipsychotics can address underlying neurobiological factors.

Understanding that ODD is rooted in organic factors is crucial. By recognizing these underlying neurological mechanisms, parents and professionals can better support children grappling with this condition.

BUILDING SOCIAL SKILLS AND EMOTIONAL INTELLIGENCE

Fostering social abilities and emotional intelligence in children with ODD can be challenging and sensitive. For these young individuals, grasping social nuances and handling their emotions might be more complex than their counterparts. Nevertheless, they can acquire these crucial life skills with guidance and tailored interventions.

A key element in enhancing social skills and emotional intelligence for children with ODD is establishing a secure and nurturing environment. This encompasses promoting open dialogue and shared understanding among relatives, educators, and healthcare providers. Parents can help children feel more inclined to participate in activities that foster their social and emotional growth by creating a setting where children feel acknowledged and cherished.

A highly effective strategy involves seamlessly incorporating social skills training into the child's daily routine. By focusing on specific areas like honing effective communication, fostering empathy, and nurturing problem-solving skills, children with ODD can steadily build the confidence to navigate social situations more adeptly. Engaging in role-playing exercises and using real-life scenarios can serve as invaluable tools to facilitate the acquisition and practical application of these essential skills.

In addition, guiding children with ODD to regulate their emotions and become more self-aware is crucial. Motivating them to constructively recognize and convey their emotions can enhance emotional intelligence. Methods like deep-breathing exercises, journaling, and mindfulness practices can play a significant role in aiding children to control their emotions and gain a deeper understanding of their feelings.

Parents, educators, and healthcare professionals must demonstrate suitable social conduct and emotional regulation alongside focused interventions. Like all children, children with ODD learn by observing the grown-ups in their lives. Healthy communication, empathy, and emotional restraint can offer invaluable examples for children with ODD.

Moreover, positive reinforcement and commendation can encourage social skills and emotional intelligence in children with ODD. By recognizing and rewarding their endeavors, caregivers can inspire children to persist in honing these essential abilities. Establishing achievable objectives and acknowledging progress can also enhance their self-esteem and determination.

For comprehensive guidance on teaching emotional regulation to parents and children while managing explosive behavior, I highly recommend referring to "Defusing Explosive Behavior." This invaluable resource introduces the PEACE method, a structured approach designed to effectively navigate challenging situations calmly and empathetically. It equips parents and children with the tools to nurture a more harmonious relationship. It encourages social skills and emotional intelligence in children with ODD through positive reinforcement and commendation.

By recognizing and celebrating their efforts, caregivers can motivate children to persist in developing these vital abilities. Furthermore, the book underscores the significance of establishing achievable objectives and acknowledging progress, enhancing self-esteem and determination in children with ODD. "Defusing Explosive Behavior" is a comprehensive guide for families looking to address the challenges of ODD and work together towards a more harmonious future.

Joining forces with mental health specialists, such as therapists and counselors, can offer insight and direction in devising customized strategies to meet the distinct needs of children with ODD. This assistance can lead to a holistic approach encompassing the child, family, educational institution, and community.

Cultivating social skills and emotional intelligence for children with ODD is a multifaceted process that entails fostering a supportive atmosphere, delivering targeted interventions, exemplifying suitable behavior, and teaming up with mental health experts. By adopting these methods, caregivers can assist children with ODD in developing the necessary resources to flourish in their social and emotional lives.

REFLECTION SECTION

1. Pause for a minute to ponder what you have learned about the possible organic reason for your child's ODD behavior. How does this understanding alter how you contemplate your child's activities?

2. In what ways do you feel that you could work on your parenting or home climate to more readily uphold your child's neurobiological requirements? Record three significant advances you can take to establish a steadier climate.

3. Consider whether drugs may be a reasonable choice for your child. What are your perspectives and worries about drugs? Record them on paper and examine them with your child's medical care supplier.

4. Reflect on the potential benefits of CBT, DBT, and other problem-solving components for your child. How might these techniques help your child develop coping, social, and essential skills? Use these approaches to write down one specific skill or behavior you would like to work on with your child.

5. Contemplate the role of self-regulation and executive function in your child's ODD behavior. How can you support your child in developing these skills? Jot down one particular activity or exercise you can engage in with your child to help them practice self-regulation and executive function.

STORY

As Ethan embarked on his preschool journey, Emily's concerns reached new heights. His temper tantrums intensified, creating hurdles in his interactions with other children. His defiance, once confined to home, now spilled over into his relationships with peers and teachers. While part of Emily hoped this was merely a passing phase, her instincts strongly suggested otherwise. She delved into research, seeking to unravel the complexities of Oppositional Defiant Disorder (ODD) and its potential connection to Ethan's behavior.

Emily observed how, in the preschool environment, Ethan struggled to follow instructions and often engaged in power struggles with his teachers. His frequent outbursts left her both puzzled and powerless. This prompted her to delve deeper into comprehending the inner workings of her son's mind.

This realization underscored the fact that children with ODD aren't necessarily devoid of logic. They may even recognize the harmful nature of their conduct, yet require support to quell intrusive thoughts and soothe the turbulent emotions that drive their behavior.

SUMMARY OF WHAT'S IN THE MIND OF A CHILD WITH ODD

ODD affects the brain's reward system and executive function. The reward system governs emotions and the experience of pleasure, encompassing dopamine release. This system may be overactive or underactive in children with ODD, resulting in challenges regulating emotions and actions.

Moreover, the maturation of the prefrontal cortex in children with ODD might not unfold as expected, impacting vital processes such as planning, decision-making, and impulse control.

These neural influences can result in various behaviors connected to ODD, like stubbornness, aggression, and impatience.

Children with ODD may have difficulty abiding by rules and respecting authority figures; they may easily get annoyed or exasperated and struggle to acknowledge responsibility for their actions.

PARENTAL SELF-ASSESSMENT: EXPLORING POTENTIAL CONTRIBUTING FACTORS

1. Have I consistently set boundaries and consequences for my child's behavior?

2. Have I provided a stable and nurturing environment for my child?

3. Have I looked for professional assistance and support for my child's behavior?

4. Have I communicated with my child, using encouraging feedback and compassion to address their behavior?

5. Have I considered environmental factors, such as family stress, injury, or changes that might contribute to my child's behavior?

Answering these questions can assist you with identifying areas where you might need to concentrate your endeavors in addressing your child's behavior and seeking support from professionals and assets in your community.

THE IMPORTANCE OF STUDYING THE MYTHS ABOUT ODD

In today's world, overflowing with information, misconceptions, and myths can easily emerge, particularly regarding subjects like ODD. Unraveling and debunking these misunderstandings is crucial to fostering a compassionate and knowledgeable perspective on ODD, which can profoundly influence the lives of those affected with the disorder and their families and communities.

Examining the myths about ODD is important for various reasons. First and foremost, it helps people recognize incorrect information, preventing the perpetuation of stereotypes or stigmatization of individuals with the disorder. Challenging misconceptions fosters a more inclusive and compassionate environment for children with ODD and their families.

Dispelling misconceptions allows families and professionals to pinpoint and apply effective treatment strategies. Myths might lead to misguided interventions or even hesitation to seek assistance, negatively impacting the child's well-being and the family's overall stability. Grasping the facts about ODD is essential for making informed decisions regarding the most suitable course of action for a child's treatment and support.

In addition, exploring myths about ODD can facilitate open, honest conversations within communities. Disputing these inaccuracies creates a secure environment where caregivers, educators, and experts can come together, discuss their encounters, swap knowledge, and gain from each other's experiences. This cooperative approach can be especially valuable in building a comprehensive support network for those affected by ODD.

Challenging misconceptions and myths about ODD can play a role in destigmatizing mental health issues more broadly. By nurturing a culture of understanding and acceptance, you make it feasible to dismantle barriers and motivate individuals to seek more help for themselves or their loved ones.

Scrutinizing the myths about ODD can result in a deeper comprehension of the disorder, propelling future research and advancements in treatment. By examining false beliefs, researchers are encouraged to investigate new paths and explore groundbreaking approaches to managing and supporting those with ODD. As a result, this creates opportunities for better outcomes and a more gratifying existence for those touched by the disorder.

In simple terms, exploring and correcting the misunderstandings about ODD is crucial. This effort can significantly impact the lives of those dealing with the disorder, their loved ones, and the community. By clearing up these misconceptions, encouraging open conversations, and creating an environment of understanding and acceptance, we can build a more inclusive and compassionate world for people with ODD. Additionally, dispelling ODD myths can reduce the stigma around mental health problems and encourage more research, which benefits society's overall well-being.

3

DON'T BE FOOLED

I believe that life is chaotic, a jumble of accidents, ambitions, misconceptions, bold intentions, lazy happenstances, and unintended consequences, yet I also believe that there are connections that illuminate our world, revealing its endless mystery and wonder.

— DAVID MARANISS

Do you consider yourself to be familiar with ODD? Be not deceived. We can go in the wrong direction because of the stigma and misunderstandings associated with this condition. It is time to make things plain and dispel any misunderstandings.

MISCONCEPTIONS SURROUNDING ODD

Many misconceptions about ODD can cause miscommunication and stigma.

Misconception: ODD is just normal childhood behavior.

Real Insight: One common misconception about ODD is that it is a commonplace childhood behavior. Parents and educators might rush to dismiss a child's defiant or forceful behavior as a stage or a part of growing up. Be that as it may, this can be dangerous as it delays getting a legitimate diagnosis and treatment for the child.

ODD is a genuine mental disorder that requires legitimate diagnosis and treatment. It is characterized by a perpetually bad-tempered mood, argumentative or defiant behavior, and vindictiveness that endures for no less than six months. It isn't simply occasional disobedience or defiance but rather a consistent and ongoing pattern of behavior that disrupts daily life.

Contrary to common misconceptions, ODD is not caused by poor parenting. ODD is largely a neurological condition, while external factors, including family conflict, inconsistent punishment, and abuse, can influence how it develops. This indicates that it has to do with the brain's information-processing mechanisms, notably those that deal with impulse control, emotional regulation, and concentration.

Misconception: ODD is linked to lower intelligence levels.

Real Insight: In reality, intelligence levels among individuals with ODD span a broad spectrum. There is no inherent connection between the presence of ODD and a person's intellectual capacity. Some individuals with ODD may excel academically and display high levels of cognitive abilities, while others may face challenges in these areas. ODD primarily revolves around patterns of defiant, argumentative, and challenging behaviors rather than intellectual prowess.

It's important to recognize that ODD affects individuals from all walks of life and with diverse cognitive abilities. Assuming a connection between ODD and lower intelligence levels is not only inaccurate but can also perpetuate stereotypes and hinder a deeper understanding of the disorder. By dispelling this misconception, we can foster a more empathetic and informed perspective on ODD and support individuals in a more inclusive and effective manner.

Misconception: ODD is caused by bad parenting.

Real Insight: According to researchers, ODD is believed to be a multifactorial disorder, which means that it results from a confluence of genetic, neurological, and environmental components (Ghosh et al., 2017). Parenting and the family environment might influence a child's behavior and increase

ODD side effects. Yet, they are not the disorder's only outcomes.

Children with ODD, studies show, frequently have altered brain chemistry, including prefrontal cortical abnormalities and changes to the dopamine reward system. These brain variations could affect the self-regulation and impulsive issues that characterize ODD (Matthys et al., 2012).

It is crucial to understand that ODD is a legitimate disorder that calls for medical evaluation and treatment and that criticizing parents for their children's actions can be demeaning and counterproductive. Parents and other caregivers can help their children by seeking the right attention and assistance if they know the complicated nature of ODD and its underlying causes.

Misconception: Children with ODD are always angry and aggressive.

Real Insight: This is a typical misunderstanding of children with ODD. Although ODD frequently manifests as anger and aggression, it's crucial to remember that not all children with the disorder display these traits. Some children with ODD may engage in passive-aggressive actions, including stubbornness, willfully breaking rules, or challenging adults.

Understanding that every child might display distinct side effects of ODD is vital because the illness is mind-boggling and has a wide variety of side effects and behaviors. It is also crucial to recall that ODD can co-occur with other diseases like ADHD or anxiety, which could affect how a child presents their side effects.

Misconception: ODD is an unchangeable, lifelong disorder, dooming those affected to a lifetime of difficulties.

Real Insight: While Oppositional Defiant Disorder can present significant challenges, many children with ODD can effectively manage and even overcome their symptoms with the right intervention and support. With early recognition and appropriate guidance, they can go on to lead fulfilling, successful lives, proving that there is hope and potential for positive change.

Misconception: ODD can be easily treated with medication alone.

Real Insight: Some parents might anticipate that medicine will quickly solve their child's behavioral issues.

While medication can be a useful component of treatment for certain children with ODD, it's anything but a fix-all. Studies have shown that medication isn't generally as compelling as behavioral interventions in treating ODD (*How Do I,* 2017). Medication is often used with behavioral therapy, like CBT and DBT, to address explicit side effects, such as anxiety or depression, that may co-occur with ODD.

Parent training as part of behavioral treatment can help ODD children improve communication and critical thinking, reduce disruptive behaviors, and develop appropriate behaviors and coping skills. Parent training is crucial to behavioral therapy because it teaches parents how to effectively manage their child's conduct at home and in other contexts. It has been proven effective in ODD therapy (Corcoran, 2003).

Thus, while medication can be useful in reducing ODD side effects, it is no longer a replacement for in-depth behavioral treatment and parent education.

Misconception: Children with ODD can control their behavior if they want to.

Real Insight: Children with Oppositional Defiant Disorder (ODD) often struggle to control their behavior, not because they don't want to, but because their condition affects their ability to do so. ODD is characterized by negative, hostile, and defiant behavior, including frequent temper tantrums, arguments with adults, and a refusal to comply with rules or requests.

Imagine their emotional "brakes" aren't working as effectively as they should. While they may have moments of self-control, their condition makes it challenging to sustain this control consistently, especially in stressful or emotionally charged situations. It's not a matter of choice but a manifestation of their mental health condition.

Misconception: Children with ODD will outgrow the disorder.

Real Insight: It is a common misconception that ODD is a stage that children will eventually outgrow. While certain children might experience reduced side effects after some time, many need ongoing help to manage their behavior.

ODD can persevere into adulthood without appropriate treatment and lead to other mental health issues, such as substance misuse and conduct disorder.

If left untreated, ODD can have serious long-term consequences. Children with untreated ODD are at increased hazard of developing other mental health disorders, like anxiety, depression, and substance misuse. Additionally, ODD is a common forerunner to conduct disorder. This more serious and disruptive behavior disorder can continue into adulthood. Legitimate treatment and intervention, including therapy and parent training, can prevent these negative results.

Misconception: ODD only affects boys.

Real Insight: ODD is often linked with boys, making it seem like it's a male-only issue. Girls are also diagnosed with ODD, although they might be less likely to get diagnosed with it. One reason is that girls with ODD may display different symptoms, like less obvious aggression and defiance. Additionally, girls with ODD might be more inclined to show passive-aggressive behavior, such as purposefully forgetting things or doing tasks inefficiently to annoy others.

Both boys and girls can have ODD but may show different signs. Parents and healthcare providers must recognize ODD symptoms in both genders to provide proper care and support.

Misconception: ODD is not a serious disorder.

Real Insight: ODD stigma and misconceptions might prevent people from realizing how severe the illness is. A common misunderstanding is that ODD is not a serious illness but a major error.

ODD can significantly influence a child's daily life and functioning. Children with ODD may experience issues in school and struggle to maintain healthy relationships with relatives and friends. The disorder can also lead to other mental health issues, like anxiety and depression, as well as substance misuse and conduct disorder.

Without proper intervention, ODD can hinder a child's potential success. Studies indicate that children with ODD face a greater risk of academic setbacks, misconduct, and challenges in sustaining employment (Kyeva et al., 2021).

It is essential to recognize the seriousness of ODD and look for appropriate diagnosis and treatment for affected children. A combination of medication, therapy, and parent training can successfully manage the disorder and improve a child's overall functioning.

Misconception: Punishment and strict discipline are the most effective ways to manage ODD.

Real Insight: While it might seem logical to tackle defiant behavior with strict discipline and punishment, research shows that this approach can often exacerbate the issues associated with Oppositional Defiant Disorder (ODD). We will go over this specific topic later on in this book.

Misconception: Children with ODD are just being difficult on purpose.

Real Insight: One of the most pervasive myths regarding ODD is that children who have it attempt to be difficult or disrespectful on purpose. Research has demonstrated that ODD is a perplexing condition influenced by biological, environmental, and psychological variables (Wilson, 2019). Children with ODD may have trouble controlling their emotions and conduct, which can result in irresponsible and rebellious behavior.

ODD is a disorder that influences a child's capacity to direct their emotions and behavior. While children with ODD may seem, by all accounts, to be intentionally difficult, they often struggle to control their impulses and respond fittingly to social situations. This can bring about defiance, argument, and refusal to follow rules or demands, which can be mistaken for intentional misbehavior.

Some medical professionals are convinced that children with ODD have differences in brain construction and function that might contribute to their behavior (Amen, n.d.). Additionally, studies have found that children with ODD may experience issues with emotional regulation, which can contribute to their challenging behaviors (Mitchison et al., 2020). Therefore, parents and guardians must approach their child's behavior with understanding and look for fitting treatment to assist the child with learning successful coping techniques.

Misconception: ODD is an uncommon disorder.

Real Insight: Contrary to popular belief, ODD affects a substantial percentage of children and adolescents, ranging from approximately 2 to 16% (*Oppositional Defiant Disorder,* 2022).

Misconception: ODD is always caused by trauma or abuse.

Real Insight: Some individuals could think that abuse or trauma has contributed to the disease. This isn't always the case, though. ODD is multifactorial, which means that while traumatic events can play a role in its development, there are typically a number of other factors at play.

While horrendous mishaps and mishandling can contribute to ODD's development, they are not always the sole reason. Research has shown that various factors, including genetics, brain science, and environment, can also play a part in the development of ODD (Wilson, 2019).

Genetic factors can make a few children more vulnerable to developing ODD. Children with a family background of conduct disorder or ODD are bound to develop the disorder themselves. Brain science also plays a part in the development of ODD.

In summary, it's vital to recognize that while injuries and mistreatment can contribute to Oppositional Defiant Disorder (ODD), it is a multifaceted condition shaped by many influences. Effectively addressing it requires a comprehensive evaluation and a holistic approach to treatment.

REFLECTING AND PLANNING: INSIGHTS FROM "DON'T BE FOOLED"

To ponder what you have learned from the chapter "Don't be Fooled" and to outline their next advances, you can use the following alternative prompts:

- What were some misunderstandings or stigmas about ODD that you had before delving into this section? How have your perceptions evolved?
- Which essential insights from this section do you feel other parents need to be aware of?

- What are common triggers or situations that appear to elicit your child's ODD behaviors? How can you proactively tackle these triggers or situations in the future?
- Which strategies or methods have effectively managed your child's ODD behaviors? How can you weave these techniques into your everyday life?
- What challenges have you faced while advocating for your child's needs in educational settings or elsewhere? How can you overcome these challenges moving forward?
- What self-care habits have been beneficial for you when dealing with the stress and complexities of parenting a child with ODD? How can you ensure these practices remain a priority?

Parents may use these prompts as an initial step for journaling or reflecting on their experiences with ODD and planning their upcoming actions to support their child's requirements.

STORY

Emily decided to seek advice from friends and family as she observed Ethan's behavior becoming increasingly concerning. However, many of them dismissed her concerns, attributing Ethan's actions to typical childhood behavior. Emily knew deep down that there was more to it, but she was often met with misconceptions about ODD. She recognized that to truly understand and address Ethan's behavior, she needed to break through these myths.

Despite her family's well-meaning advice, Emily couldn't shake the feeling that Ethan's conduct was different from typical childhood defiance. It puzzled her that, as she delved into her research, there were signs of ADHD as well, further confusing the diagnosis. She found herself in conversations with well-intentioned friends, explaining that it wasn't merely a matter of setting firmer boundaries. She knew that to help her son, they needed to uncover the truth about ODD.

THE IMPORTANCE OF NEW PERSPECTIVES

One of the reasons why we need a different viewpoint when it comes to ODD is to challenge these misconceptions. By looking at the disorder from a different angle, we can better understand the main drivers, side effects, and viable treatments for ODD. We can also learn how to help children with ODD in more powerful and compassionate ways.

Additionally, taking a different viewpoint can assist us in empathizing with children who have ODD and their families. Blaming or judging a child's behavior may be easy without considering the underlying issues contributing to their challenges. By stepping into the shoes of someone with ODD or their parental figure, we can gain a new appreciation for their battles and work toward creating a stronger and more inclusive environment for them.

In conclusion, having a different point of view on ODD can assist us with challenging misconceptions, gaining a better understanding of the disorder, and feeling for those affected by it. This can lead to additional successful treatments, better results for children with ODD, and a more compassionate and inclusive society.

4

A NEW PERSPECTIVE

You've done it before, and you can do it now. See the positive possibilities. Redirect the substantial energy of your frustration and turn it into positive, effective, unstoppable determination.

— RALPH MARSTON

Have you, at any point, considered ODD as a blessing in disguise? In this part, you will discover how a new viewpoint can transform how you approach ODD and reveal its hidden potential.

Understanding that ODD is a mental health issue capable of causing significant distress and hindering daily life is crucial.

However, individuals with ODD also exhibit potential benefits and positive characteristics. With appropriate assistance and encouragement, their strengths can be further developed.

- **Creativity**

Children with ODD can be challenging for parents, guardians, and educators. In any case, it's important to note that children with ODD also have potential strengths. One such strength is their innovativeness. Research has shown that children with ODD tend to have better divergent thinking skills than their friends without the disorder (Abraham & Studaker-Cordner, 2012).

The ability to produce numerous ideas and think beyond conventional boundaries is known as divergent thinking. It requires stepping away from habitual thought patterns and devising original solutions to problems. Such a thought process is an essential element of creativity, which can be beneficial in everyday situations, from education and work to interpersonal relationships.

While young individuals with ODD may frequently question authority and resist structure, their creative potential can be cultivated and supported through appropriate intervention and guidance. This may entail promoting creative pursuits like art, music, and expressive writing. Additionally, it may involve integrating imaginative thinking into academic endeavors and problem-solving activities. Recognizing and nurturing the inventive spirits of children with ODD allows parents, guardians, and teachers to support the development of their unique strengths and possibly enhance their general well-being.

Adopting a well-rounded strategy when interacting with children affected by ODD is paramount. Challenges posed by the disorder notwithstanding, it's vital to identify these individuals' inherent abilities, such as their creative talents. Children with ODD can refine their strengths through appropriate assistance and encouragement and potentially experience fulfilling lives.

- **Strong will**

One remarkable strength among those with ODD is their strong will. Children with ODD exhibit remarkable independence, determination, and persistence, even in adversity.

Research has shown that individuals with ODD are more likely to champion their peers against bullying, stand up for their rights, seek justice in unjust situations, and take on leadership roles (Angoff, n.d.). This strong willpower can be a tremendous asset. It can lead to resilience, determination, and an unwavering commitment to their goals.

While this strong will may sometimes pose challenges, especially in the context of treatment, as individuals with ODD may resist authority and find it difficult to accept help, this formidable determination, and willpower can be channeled toward positive actions and outcomes with the right guidance and support. It allows individuals with ODD to persevere through difficulties and overcome obstacles, ultimately helping them flourish and make a positive impact on their lives and the lives of others.

- **Independence**

Individuals with Oppositional Defiant Disorder (ODD) often display a remarkable inclination for self-sufficiency and autonomy, which can be channeled to yield highly favorable outcomes. While this innate desire for independence may sometimes manifest as defiance or opposition to authority, it also lays the foundation for developing robust self-assurance and exceptional decision-making skills.

With the right guidance and encouragement, children with ODD can learn to harness their self-reliance positively, ultimately blossoming into remarkably self-sufficient adults. Research has consistently shown that children with ODD frequently exhibit elevated levels of confidence, determination, and perseverance, even in the face of significant challenges (Angoff, n.d.).

This strong willpower can be a remarkable asset if appropriately nurtured and directed. For example, with the guidance and support of caring adults, children with ODD can channel their determination towards achieving uplifting goals and consistently exercising sound judgment.

- **Persistence**

Children with ODD frequently exhibit impressive determination, which can be advantageous when steered positively. Such persistence may reveal itself in various forms, including an unshakable dedication to an endeavor or an uncompromising drive to achieve a specific goal. With appropriate assistance and direction, it can be redirected toward beneficial actions and outcomes.

For instance, children with ODD who are instructed to set feasible goals and persistently pursue them might develop a strong sense of self-viability and personal achievement. This can lead to improved confidence and overall prosperity. Additionally, when children with ODD learn to persistently pursue positive behaviors and results, they may develop stronger social abilities and relationships.

While persistence can sometimes manifest as defiance or opposition to authority in children with ODD, with the right guidance and backing, it tends to be harnessed as a positive quality and used to accomplish personal and social goals.

- **Assertiveness**

Assertiveness is a quality that involves the capacity to communicate one's needs, opinions, and feelings reasonably and confidently without infringing on the privileges of others. Individuals with ODD may display elevated degrees of assertiveness, as they tend to have a strong sense of self and are not afraid to offer their viewpoints and feelings. This characteristic can be harnessed and nurtured with suitable treatment and backing.

Notwithstanding, this assertiveness is often expressed negatively, like argumentativeness and antagonism toward others. With the right guidance and backing, individuals with ODD can learn to communicate their assertiveness positively, for example, advocating for themselves and others, negotiating conflict, and standing up for what they have confidence in.

Several techniques can be used to advance healthy assertiveness in individuals with ODD. One technique is to show them how to communicate their thoughts reasonably and concisely using "I" statements. This involves expressing their feelings and needs without blaming or attacking others. Another technique assists them with developing critical thinking abilities, which can increase their capacity to communicate successfully and decisively in challenging situations.

It is also important to note that assertiveness differs from aggression or defiance. While assertiveness involves expressing oneself confidently and clearly, aggression involves behavior intended to hurt or intimidate others. Defiance involves refusing to consent to rules or demands and behaving without regard for the feelings or needs of others. Therefore, it is important to show individuals with ODD the difference between assertiveness and aggression or defiance and to assist them with learning to put themselves out there positively and productively.

- **Leadership skills**

Children with ODD often exhibit natural leadership qualities such as decisiveness and a strong desire for control. These traits can be powerful when channeled effectively. In this context, leadership is about influencing and guiding others toward common goals, and children with ODD have the potential for this. However, negative behaviors can obscure these abilities if not managed properly.

Effective leadership isn't about forcefulness but encompasses compassion, emotional intelligence, and genuine communication. Nurturing these skills in children with ODD is essential. Creating opportunities to take on leadership roles in various settings, including home, school, and community organizations, can foster their development as leaders.

Guidance from trusted mentors can play a vital role in helping children with ODD channel their innate leadership skills constructively. These mentors can provide direction support, and teach emotional awareness and compassion— crucial components of effective leadership. With the right guidance, children with ODD can learn to control negative behaviors and use their positive traits to become successful leaders in their personal and professional lives.

- **Resilience**

Resilience can be defined as the ability to endlessly adapt to adversity and unpleasant life-changing situations. Individuals with ODD may develop more noteworthy resilience due to the challenges they face in their everyday lives. They might need to navigate difficult relational idiosyncrasies, fight in school, or face social rejection, which can all be unpleasant and overwhelming experiences. Notwithstanding these challenges, individuals with ODD may develop coping methodologies and critical thinking skills that can help them overcome future hindrances.

Youngsters affected by ODD might exhibit enhanced emotional resilience compared to peers not facing the condition. This resilience could stem from encountering and surmounting hurdles, fostering a sense of self-efficacy and assurance. Close bonds with adults, such as parents, teachers, or mental health experts, can further aid ODD-affected children in honing their coping skills and establishing positive coping strategies.

Despite resilience being a valuable trait, it's vital to recognize that ODD can still negatively impact an individual's mental well-being and accomplishments. To address the root causes of the disorder and create effective coping techniques, seeking professional assistance and support for ODD-affected individuals and their families is essential.

In summary, due to daily difficulties, individuals with ODD may be stronger and better equipped for coping. Yet, addressing the underlying reasons for the condition is crucial, looking for professional treatment and building viable coping mechanisms to improve overall mental health and achievement.

- **Self-awareness**

Those contending with ODD often exhibit an increased self-awareness. They may be remarkably perceptive of their capabilities and limitations and keenly understand their emotional reactions to various situations. Leveraging this refined self-awareness can empower individuals with ODD to adjust their actions and interactions.

When people with ODD recognize their emotional triggers, they can strive to control their responses and adopt more beneficial behaviors. For instance, if an individual with ODD knows they are prone to anger when faced with challenges, they can acquire techniques to manage their frustration and communicate it more effectively.

Moreover, self-awareness can contribute to an enriched understanding and empathy toward others. When individuals with ODD become aware of their emotional responses, they may cultivate an increased attentiveness to the emotions and needs of others. This refined sensitivity can lead to improved communication and stronger relationships.

Self-awareness is a valuable quality that individuals with ODD possess. This quality can be channeled with guidance to encourage positive behaviors and connections. Therapeutic interventions and other treatments can assist those with ODD in developing a more profound self-awareness and emotional regulation aptitude, leading to better outcomes in both personal and professional spheres.

- **Advocacy**

Individuals with ODD must often navigate challenging situations, tapping into their inner strengths to develop necessary skills. These skills enable them to assert their needs and effectively communicate their feelings, even under difficult circumstances. With the right guidance and support, people with ODD can direct their advocacy skills toward positive outcomes for themselves and others.

Advocacy is a crucial skill for individuals with ODD, as it helps them maneuver through intricate systems and access required resources. Young people who receive training in advocacy skills significantly improve their ability to access services and genuinely convey their needs to authority figures (Dietzman, n.d.).

Additionally, individuals with ODD may be more likely to resist injustice and champion the rights of themselves and others.

In summary, advocacy skills can be a valuable asset for individuals with ODD, helping them assert their needs, navigate complex systems, and foster positive community changes. With the appropriate support and guidance, people with ODD can develop and enhance these skills for use in various personal and professional settings.

PROMOTING INCLUSIVITY AND UNDERSTANDING OF ODD

Establishing an inviting and sympathetic space for those impacted by ODD is crucial in improving the lives of the children, their loved ones, educators, and the surrounding community. Potential hindrances to their joy and accomplishments can be dismantled by forging a caring and supportive atmosphere.

A vital element in encouraging inclusivity and appreciation of ODD involves delivering education and spreading correct information about the disorder and its traits, aiding in dispelling falsehoods and nurturing a more empathetic viewpoint. This educational endeavor should encompass parents, teachers, and other specialists who engage with children and society. Knowledge is the bedrock for empathy and acceptance. Delaying precise information about ODD and its impact on children and families is crucial.

It's important to emphasize that by being empathetic and sympathetic to provide a space where your child feels safe does not mean that they are not at fault and do not need to take responsibility for their actions. Instead, it opens the door to teaching them how to learn from their mistakes and make better choices in the future, rather than subjecting them to consistent punishment.

Within the educational realm, teachers and school administrators are central to promoting inclusivity for children with ODD. Schools can develop an environment where every child can flourish by adopting suitable strategies and accommodations to assist these students. This might entail specialized training for educators, tailored education plans, and allocating resources such as counseling services or peer support initiatives. By addressing the requirements of students with ODD, schools convey a robust message of acceptance and understanding to the entire educational community.

Another vital element of encouraging inclusivity and comprehension of ODD is giving voice to those directly impacted by the disorder. Empowering children with ODD and their families to recount their experiences can offer priceless insights into their obstacles and the most helpful support. These personal accounts can be potent instruments for debunking misconceptions and stereotypes about ODD and fostering a more empathetic and inclusive attitude.

Moreover, cooperation is fundamental in cultivating inclusivity for children with ODD. Parents, teachers, healthcare professionals, and community members should collaborate to form a support network tailored to the distinct needs of children with the disorder. This partnership can enable the exchange of resources and know-how, which can be indispensable in advancing understanding and inclusive practices.

It is imperative to recognize the talents and accomplishments of children with ODD. Celebrating their triumphs and contributions makes it possible to challenge the adverse assumptions frequently associated with the disorder and foster a more optimistic and inclusive view of these children and their potential.

Advocating for inclusivity and understanding ODD necessitates a diverse approach that incorporates education, collaboration, and the acknowledgment of the exceptional strengths and experiences of those affected by the disorder. By collectively creating a more compassionate and supportive milieu, the lives of children with ODD can be enriched, enabling them to achieve their full potential.

FINANCIAL PLANNING AND ODD

When addressing this disorder, emphasis is often placed on the emotional and psychological elements of the condition. Nevertheless, it's vital to consider the financial consequences that ODD can impose on a family. Financial planning for families with a child diagnosed with ODD might appear daunting. Still, it is an essential component of ensuring long-lasting stability and support.

It's crucial to acknowledge that the expenses linked to treating and managing ODD can be considerable. These costs may include therapy sessions, medication, supplementary educational resources, or tutoring. Families must evaluate their financial status and devise a budget that accommodates these expenses while also considering potential changes in treatment plans or unanticipated costs.

One approach to prepare for the financial implications of ODD is to create an emergency fund. This fund can be a fallback in case of unexpected costs or shifts in the family's financial circumstances. By allocating a portion of the family's earnings, they can feel more secure knowing that resources are available to tackle any sudden financial challenges that may emerge.

Families should also investigate various financial aid programs and resources alongside setting up an emergency fund. Numerous government agencies, non-profit organizations, and private foundations extend support to families with children diagnosed with ODD or other behavioral disorders. Examining these programs and applying for aid can help alleviate some of the financial pressures tied to ODD treatment.

Another vital aspect of financial planning for families grappling with ODD is comprehending the potential influence of the disorder on the child's future earning capacity. While many children with ODD can surmount the difficulties associated with the disorder and lead accomplished, satisfying lives, others may have trouble with long-term employment or require ongoing support.

Furthermore, families must inform themselves about the tax ramifications of ODD-related expenses. Sometimes, families might be eligible for tax deductions or credits relating to their child's medical costs or educational assistance. Seeking advice from a tax professional or financial planner can offer valuable guidance on optimizing these benefits and minimizing the financial strain on the family.

Transparent communication is crucial when tackling the financial challenges associated with ODD. Families should continuously discuss their financial situation and collaborate to develop a plan that suits their needs. By cultivating a supportive and cooperative atmosphere, families can more effectively navigate the intricacies of financial planning and ODD.

Financial planning for families dealing with ODD is a critical yet frequently neglected aspect of managing the disorder. By devising a budget, creating an emergency fund, researching financial aid programs, contemplating long-term consequences, and sustaining open communication, families can better prepare for the financial challenges that may surface and ensure a more stable and supportive environment for their child with ODD.

SELF-ANALYSIS QUESTIONNAIRE FOR PARENTS MANAGING A CHILD WITH ODD

1. Describe how your child's ODD has challenged you and your family.
2. How has reading Chapter 4 affected your understanding of ODD? Jot down one illustration.
3. Decide on one quality that your ODD-affected child has that stands out. How can you promote and help this quality?
4. Consider a recent occasion when your ODD-affected child displayed challenging conduct. What feelings did you experience at that time? What was your reaction?
5. Make a note of one technique you use to control your anxiety and irritation when coping with your child's ODD.

6. What role does empathy play in managing ODD? Describe one way to show empathy toward your child during a difficult situation.

7. How can you encourage creativity in an ODD child? Note one thing you did or thought of.

8. What exactly does having a strong will mean? How can you encourage your child to constructively use their strong will?

9. Pick one situation where you can interact with your ODD child more self-awarely.

10. What is one concrete step you can take to be an advocate for your child with ODD based on what you learned in Chapter 4?

STORY

Undeterred, Emily sought professional help for Ethan. After several evaluations, they received a diagnosis of ODD. While it was challenging to accept, Emily felt a sense of relief knowing what they were dealing with. Armed with this new perspective, she was determined to find ways to support her son.

With the diagnosis in hand, Emily began to understand that Ethan's behavior wasn't his fault. It was a condition they could work through together. Emily was more determined than ever to help her son navigate the challenges that ODD presented.

INTERACTIVE ELEMENT:

It is essential to remember that every child possesses strengths and positive attributes that should be celebrated and nurtured.

Take a moment to compile a list of your child's strong points. What are their areas of excellence? What are their positive traits? What activities do they enjoy participating in? Once you have identified these strengths, consider how you can build upon them. How can you encourage and support your child in these areas? How can you help them employ their strong suits to overcome challenges in other aspects?

By zeroing in on your child's assets and expanding on them, you can assist them with fostering a positive identity and trust in their capacities. Remember that each child is extraordinary and brings something uniquely amazing to the world.

HOW DO WE COPE WITH A CHILD WITH ODD?

It can be overwhelming and sometimes frustrating when navigating the challenges of parenting a child with ODD. However, it's essential to remember that you're not alone in this, and there are effective ways to manage the situation.

One of the most crucial steps you can take is to seek professional help. A mental health expert, such as a therapist or psychologist, can provide invaluable assistance in helping both you and your child develop coping strategies and foster a positive relationship.

One key action is to learn as much as possible about ODD. Doing so helps in understanding a child's behavior, making it easier to find ways to handle it. It might be helpful to join a support group for parents with children with ODD, connecting with others facing similar circumstances.

Lastly, keep the focus on positive aspects. Building on a child's strengths can nurture a supportive relationship and create a foundation for behavior management. Always celebrate their achievements, big or small, and give them praise and encouragement for good behavior.

With time, patience, and the right strategies, navigating the challenges of raising a child with ODD and supporting their growth and well-being is possible.

7-STEP PLAN FOR PEACE

It is easier to build strong children than to repair broken men.

— FREDERICK DOUGLASS

D oes it seem like you constantly walk on eggshells around your child with ODD? Are you tired of the endless power struggles and arguments? It is time to regain control and create a peaceful home environment. This chapter delves into a 7-step plan that equips you with the tools and techniques to tackle ODD challenges and lay the groundwork for harmonious daily living. Get ready to bid farewell to chaos and welcome serenity.

Enhance your journey in implementing the 7-step plan to peace by delving into our "Defusing a Child with ODD Workbook." This comprehensive companion offers a wealth of bonus materials, expert insights, and practical exercises to further assist you in addressing Oppositional Defiant Disorder in your child. It's your key to building a stronger, more peaceful connection within your family.

STEP 1: BUILDING A POSITIVE RELATIONSHIP WITH YOUR CHILD

Managing ODD by fostering a positive relationship that promotes open communication, mutual respect, and trust between parent and child is essential. Children with ODD often feel misunderstood, judged, and dismissed, so building strong connections helps them feel loved and supported. Spend time with your child engaging in activities they enjoy, listening to their opinions and feelings without judgment, and providing praise and positive reinforcement when appropriate.

Learning to discern between intentional and unintentional defiant behavior before disciplining your child is crucial. Kids with ODD can exhibit challenging behaviors due to anxiety, frustration, or other emotional issues. As a parent, it's important to differentiate between willful defiance and noncompliance rooted in underlying emotional problems. Responding to your child's behavior with empathy, under-standing, and support can help reduce their defiant actions.

Creating small, collaborative goals can significantly assist in reducing oppositional and defiant behaviors. Involve your child in establishing attainable objectives and motivate their efforts to reach them. Celebrate each small triumph to foster a positive outlook and a feeling of accomplishment.

Asserting your role as a parent is vital. You are not your child's friend but their caregiver, protector, mentor, and life guide. Kids with ODD often push and test limits. Hence, it's crucial to be clear about your role as a parent and establish firm boundaries and consequences for negative behaviors. Consistency in parenting and boundaries helps the child feel a sense of stability and security.

Creating moments of joy can enhance your child's mood and reduce defiant behaviors. Kids with ODD frequently struggle with low self-esteem, anxiety, and depression, leading to negative and oppositional conduct. Participating in activities your child enjoys can help build a positive relationship and reduce challenging behaviors. Here are some ideas for creating joyful moments with your child.

- **Play games:** Taking part in games provides a wonderful chance to establish a connection with your child while having fun together. Identify games that pique your child's curiosity and fit their age range. Board games, card games, and video games are all superb selections.

- **Make time to talk**: Talking to your child about their day can be a magnificent method for building a more grounded relationship. Find an opportunity to ask your child how their day went, distinguish their feelings, and examine what turned out badly or what went right that day and why. While talking with an ODD child, it's essential to impart in a non-critical manner and to effectively pay attention to what they need to say.

- **Participate in touch-based and sensory activities**: Engaging in touch-based and sensory activities can be an enjoyable and captivating way to bond with your child. Experiences such as finger painting, playing with modeling clay, and water activities can delight children and parents.

- **Find activities to bond over.** For tweens and adolescents, it very well may be challenging to find activities that they appreciate and that guardians can take part in. Finding activities you both appreciate is fundamental, like cooking, playing sports, or watching a film. Attention to your child's leisure activities and interests can strengthen your relationship.

STEP 2: SET CLEAR AND CONSISTENT EXPECTATIONS AND LIMITS

Navigating a child with ODD requires the establishment of clear, unwavering expectations and boundaries. These youngsters often test limits, making it all the more vital to create consequences that serve as lessons rather than punishments. Here are some guidelines for crafting precise and consistent expectations and boundaries.

1. **Set Clear Expectations:** Communicate in advance what is allowed and what isn't, and explain the reasons behind these expectations. This helps your child understand the importance of following rules and limits.

2. **Be Consistent:** Stick to similar routines, expectations, and outcomes every day. Consistency makes it easier for children with ODD to grasp and follow your established rules. Inconsistency can confuse them and make understanding what's expected of them difficult.

3. **Keep It Simple:** ODD children can feel overwhelmed with too many rules. Keep your guidelines straightforward. Use positive language when setting expectations, focusing on the desired behaviors rather than the undesirable ones.

4. **Stay Calm and Firm:** Avoid reacting emotionally to your child's actions, and maintain a firm yet

composed demeanor when enforcing boundaries. Responding with anger or frustration can escalate the situation and make it more challenging to manage.

5. **Offer Choices:** Children with ODD may respond better to choices than direct commands. Present them with options within the boundaries you've established. For example, ask, "Would you prefer to clean your room now or after dinner?"

6. **Apply Consequences:** When a child crosses a boundary, it's essential to implement an appropriate consequence. Consequences should be relevant, consistent, and directly related to the behavior. For instance, if a child hits a sibling, a consequence might be restitution, such as making amends with the person they hit in some way, such as picking up their toys, helping with a chore, or assisting in another task. Clearly and calmly communicate consequences and consistently follow through.

7. **Give them a voice:** It's important to recognize that some expectations may benefit from flexibility. In certain situations, allowing your child to have a say and working together to find common ground through compromise can be valuable. However, when expectations are adjusted through compromise, it's crucial to establish an agreed-upon consequence as part of the negotiation.

For example, if bedtime is a point of contention, you might negotiate a slightly later bedtime with your child. In this case, you agree on the new bedtime and the consequence if your child consistently fails to adhere to it; the bedtime will increase by 10 minutes earlier if continually not adhered to. This approach fosters a sense of shared responsibility. It reinforces the importance of meeting expectations while allowing room for flexibility when appropriate and the child to understand that their actions have consequences.

1. **Write and Publish Expectations:** Document the expectations and consequences clearly in a place accessible to everyone in the family. This written agreement serves as a visual reminder of the rules, making them more tangible and easier for everyone to understand and follow.

2. **Acknowledge Your Role:** In this collaborative effort, recognize that expectations shouldn't focus solely on your child's behavior. Include any behaviors you, as a parent, are actively working on improving. By openly acknowledging and addressing your commitments to change, you set a positive example for your child and demonstrate the importance of continuous growth and self-improvement within the family unit.

STEP 3: USE POSITIVE REINFORCEMENT TO ENCOURAGE GOOD BEHAVIOR

Positive reinforcement is a significant tool for ODD children, who are often more receptive to prizes and positive input than punishment or criticism. As discussed earlier in this book, ODD children's brains can sometimes overreact or underreact to dopamine responses, making the normalization of positive reinforcement all the more important.

Apply positive reinforcement effectively by clarifying to the child why they are rewarded for specific actions. This helps the child grasp what they are doing correctly and strengthens the desired behavior. As an illustration, you could say, "it is truly remarkable how well you tidied up your room. It demonstrates that you are responsible and capable of caring for your belongings."

By using positive reinforcement in this way, you not only encourage positive behavior but also provide the child with valuable feedback that aids in their understanding of why their actions are deserving of praise and rewards. This approach helps manage ODD-related challenges and contributes to the child's overall development and emotional well-being.

1. **Identify desired actions:** When pinpointing desired actions, it's essential to be precise and select attainable behaviors. For instance, instead of

rewarding a child for being "good," offer incentives for completing homework without prompting or expressing feelings through words rather than acting out.

2. **Provide immediate rewards:** Swift rewards help children associate their actions with the incentive. If the reward is given too long after the behavior, they may not understand the reason for the reward. For example, if a child cleans their room, grant the incentive (such as extra screen time) immediately after they finish.

3. **Vary the incentives:** Offering a variety of incentives maintains interest and increases the likelihood that a child will respond positively to positive reinforcement. For example, verbal praise, stickers, a favorite snack, or an enjoyable activity can be rewarded.

4. **Maintain consistency:** When it comes to positive reinforcement, consistency is crucial. A child may become confused or lose motivation if rewards are sporadically or promised incentives aren't provided. Consistency in applying positive reinforcement and delivering promised rewards is essential.

5. **Acknowledge effort:** In raising a child with Oppositional Defiant Disorder (ODD), it's vital to understand that their struggles and challenges are part of their growth process. Success is not just about the end result; it's about the effort,

determination, and steps taken towards improvement. Recognizing and acknowledging these efforts sends a powerful message that their hard work is valued, regardless of the outcome.

Praising the Attempt, Not Just the Outcome

Consider a child who is struggling with reading. Instead of solely focusing on their reading ability, take a moment to applaud their determination and practice. For instance, you can say, "I'm really proud of how hard you're working on your reading. You're putting in a lot of effort, and that's fantastic!" This positive reinforcement makes the child feel valued and encourages them to persevere in their efforts.

Explore the companion guide of Defusing a Child with Oppositional Defiant Disorder Workbook for more specific ideas.

STEP 4: USE APPROPRIATE CONSEQUENCES FOR NEGATIVE BEHAVIOR

When dealing with the challenging conduct frequently displayed by children with ODD, including disobedience, hostility, and opposition, it's vital to focus on suitable consequences. This method guides the child toward improved decision-making instead of simply subjecting them to punishment.

While negative behavior may test our patience and trigger frustration, it's important to recognize these moments as potential openings for growth. Rather than reacting solely with disciplinary measures, view them as chances to connect with your child, understand the underlying causes of their actions, and guide them towards more constructive choices. You can transform challenging situations into valuable teaching moments by honing your ability to distinguish between the two. However, in instances where consequences are warranted, they must be logical, related to the unwanted behavior, and consistently applied. This approach helps address immediate issues and contributes to your child's long-term development of essential life skills and emotional resilience.

Logical consequences are more effective than punishments, as they are directly related to the behavior and make sense in the given context. These consequences should be suitable for the child's age, developmental level, and the specific behavior in question while also serving as a learning experience.

It is essential to employ rational consequences to rectify the issue rather than just penalizing the child. These consequences must be relevant to the behavior, child's age, and developmental stage. For example, if a child creates a mess, they should clean it up, helping them understand the impact of their actions and instilling a sense of responsibility.

Consistency plays a vital role when it comes to consequences. Clarify which behaviors will result in consequences and always follow through. This approach helps the child comprehend expectations and the consequences of their actions while building trust between them and the caregiver.

Steer clear of physical punishment, which can be detrimental and will worsen the situation. Instead, emphasize consequences that guide the child towards making improved choices, like temporarily losing access to a toy they mishandled, teaching them that actions have consequences, and encouraging emotional and behavioral self-regulation.

Precision in delineating consequences for specific behaviors is paramount. Take, for instance, a scenario where a child, in a fit of anger, damages an electronic device. In such cases, it may be necessary for the child to take responsibility by contributing to the cost of replacing the damaged item or temporarily forfeiting certain privileges while assisting with household chores to help alleviate the incurred expenses. The provision of precise consequences not only serves to establish a direct connection between their actions and the resulting outcomes but also fosters a deeper understanding of the cause-and-effect relationship in their behavior.

Engaging the child in determining consequences can help them assume responsibility for their actions and learn from their mistakes. Involving the child makes consequences feel less arbitrary and more meaningful, fostering problem-solving skills and accountability.

Praising effort rather than simply outcomes profoundly impacts a child's self-esteem and attitude. It helps them develop a growth mindset, believing they can improve through dedication and hard work. When they encounter challenges, they are more likely to view them as opportunities for growth rather than insurmountable obstacles.

By fostering a culture of recognizing and appreciating effort, you instill resilience and a positive attitude in your child. They become more open to learning and trying new things, knowing that their efforts are valued and celebrated. This approach not only aids in managing ODD but also sets the stage for their overall development as confident, motivated individuals.

Implementing suitable consequences for negative behavior is a crucial step in managing ODD. Logical consequences that are appropriate for the behavior, consistent, and tailored to the child's age and developmental level can effectively teach the child to make better choices. Additionally, involving the child in the process and providing positive reinforcement can help them develop a sense of accountability and promote appropriate behavior.

STEP 5: TEACH YOUR CHILD PROBLEM-SOLVING AND COPING SKILLS

A critical aspect of managing ODD behavior involves helping these children navigate their emotions, tackle challenges, and cope with stress. By imparting coping mechanisms and problem-solving skills, their ability to control their conduct can be enhanced, thus reducing the likelihood of outbursts and opposition.

1. **Embrace a fresh start every day:** It's vital to greet each day as a clean slate, leaving behind any lingering frustration over past behaviors. While your child may have faced challenges before, adopting a positive mindset and providing support and encouragement are essential in fostering positive behavior.

2. **Introduce calming methods:** Kids with ODD might struggle to manage their emotions and react appropriately to stressors. Teach them calming techniques like deep breathing, slow muscle relaxation, or mindfulness to handle stress and emotions better. Practice these methods when they're calm and not overwhelmed, building coping skills. For more techniques and in-depth guidance, check out my book, "Defusing an Explosive Child."

3. **Foster open dialogue:** ODD children may face communication challenges, leading to misunderstandings and conflicts. Encourage them to express their feelings and thoughts in a safe, supportive environment, helping them master authentic communication. By honing their communication skills, they can articulate their needs and resolve conflicts without resorting to defiance and anger.

4. **Role-play resolutions:** Children with ODD might find problem-solving difficult, resulting in frustration and outbursts. Role-playing situations with your child and helping them devise appropriate solutions can develop problem-solving skills and apply them in practice. This approach builds self-confidence and diminishes negative behaviors.

5. **Divide tasks into bite-sized steps:** ODD children might struggle to complete tasks, particularly large or complex ones. Splitting tasks into smaller, more manageable steps can reduce feelings of overwhelm and frustration. For example, tidying their room can be broken down into smaller tasks like making the bed, putting away toys, and organizing the closet. This approach helps the child feel more in control and increases their likelihood of success.

6. **Cultivate positive self-talk:** ODD children may experience low self-esteem and engage in negative self-talk. Guide them in embracing affirmative self-talk, uplifting their self-worth and certainty. Urge them to swap pessimistic notions with more optimistic ones. For example, rather than dwelling on thoughts like "I'm never going to manage this," support them in adopting the perspective of "I can achieve this if I tackle it one step at a time."

7. **Promote Self-Reflection for Positive Choices:** Help your child think about their actions and behavior, which can help them understand the results of their

decisions and make better choices in the future. Guide them in identifying situations where they might have acted impulsively or made less-than-ideal choices, and encourage them to consider alternative approaches.

This exercise aids the child in cultivating self-awareness and refining their decision-making prowess.

STEP 6: CONSIDER FAMILY-BASED THERAPY AND SUPPORT

This stage focuses on engaging everyone involved in nurturing the child's positive behavior and emotional well-being. Here are some ways to implement this step.

- **Create a United Front:** Facilitating a child's acquisition and incorporation of new behaviors requires the alignment of all adults in their lives. Various caregivers maintain consistent expectations and approaches, providing clarity for the child and promoting a more effective learning and adaptation process. Therefore, maintaining open communication with everyone involved in the child's care and education is crucial. Work together to establish consistent expectations and consequences. Suppose some family members or caregivers struggle to support the child's growth. In that case, limiting or adjusting their involvement in the child's life may be necessary until they can provide support. This decision can be challenging but prioritizes the child's well-being and provides them with the support and consistency they need.

- **Help those surrounding the child learn and exhibit improved behaviors:** In addition to maintaining consistent expectations and approaches, adults in the child's life can also model positive behaviors and coping skills for the child to learn. This can include communication skills, problem-solving strategies, and affirmative self-talk. By demonstrating these skills in their interactions with the child and one another, adults can foster a stable and uplifting environment that encourages the child's growth and development. Family-centered therapy is a potent tool in facilitating this growth process. It provides a structured and supportive setting where all family members can learn and develop together. When collaborating with a therapist, families can cultivate new skills and strategies for effective communication, problem-solving, and coping. Simultaneously, this process strengthens their connections and relationships with one another.

STEP 7: TAKE CARE OF YOURSELF AND YOUR
FAMILY

Caring for a child with ODD can be a tough and taxing journey. Guardians genuinely need to care for themselves and
their loved ones to guarantee they are in a prime situation to
help their child.

- **Organize family outings and events in safer
  environments:** Be mindful of your child's triggers
  and plan family excursions and gatherings
  accordingly. For example, if your child is agitated by
  loud noises, avoid locations with blaring music or
  crowded spaces. Choosing safer environments that
  are less likely to provoke your child can help reduce
  their anxiety and enhance the overall experience for
  everyone.
- **Carve out time for yourself and with non-ODD
  family members**: Arrange care for your ODD
  children so everyone can catch a breather. Managing
  a child with ODD can be demanding and exhausting,
  so making time for yourself and other family
  members is vital. Plan activities that allow you to
  spend quality time with your non-ODD relatives or
  indulge in some solitude. Organizing care for your
  ODD child during these periods is essential so
  everyone can enjoy a much-needed respite.

- **Allocate time for activities that bring happiness, such as working out, reading, or socializing with friends:** Looking after a child with ODD can be all-consuming, but setting aside moments for yourself and the hobbies you delight in is essential. Participating in activities you love can rejuvenate your energy and alleviate stress, ultimately fostering a positive influence on your entire family. Embrace stress-management techniques, such as mindfulness, deep breathing, or yoga, to assist in handling stress and anxiety.

Caring for a child with ODD can be challenging, so it's essential to employ these stress-management strategies for more effective coping. Mindfulness, deep breathing, and yoga are just a few stress-management practices that can assist in relaxation and managing unease. Practicing these methods can help you feel more centered and better prepared to face the challenges of caring for a child with ODD. If you find value in affirmations, consider exploring my audiobook on Audible, "*Take a Breath Mamas*," designed specifically for mothers raising neurodiverse children.

SCHOOL SUPPORT AND ACCOMMODATIONS FOR CHILDREN WITH ODD

Educational institutions hold a central place in the lives of children, and for those struggling with ODD, the support and adjustments offered can be game-changing. Ensuring that students with ODD receive the care and assistance they require to thrive is paramount, as it involves acknowledging their distinct needs and fostering a nurturing, inclusive environment. It is crucial to ensure that students with ODD receive the understanding and assistance they need to succeed, which entails recognizing their unique requirements and offering a warm, inclusive atmosphere.

A critical starting point is to devise individualized education plans (IEPs) or 504 plans tailored to the needs of children with ODD. Collaboratively developed by educators, parents, and healthcare professionals, these plans guarantee that students receive the appropriate support academically and socially (ADDitude editors, 2022). For a more in-depth guide on this topic, explore my book, "The Special Education Playbook for Parents."

One fundamental accommodation for these children involves setting consistent, unambiguous expectations. By laying out clear rules and guidelines, students with ODD can grasp what is expected of them, thereby reducing the chances of confusion. Visual aids, such as charts or lists, can be employed by teachers to emphasize these expectations and serve as reminders of the desired conduct.

Another vital accommodation revolves around offering frequent positive reinforcement. Recognizing and commending good behavior can effectively motivate children with ODD and encourage them to participate positively in the classroom. Beyond traditional rewards like stickers or points, teachers could consider granting them a unique role within the classroom, like a "helper" position, which can be highly impactful. Additionally, a small certificate or a personalized acknowledgment can be exceptionally meaningful to celebrate their achievements and contributions.

Moreover, implementing suitable consequences for unwanted behavior is essential. Teachers should avoid punitive measures that might worsen a child's ODD symptoms, opting for logical consequences that correlate directly to the misconduct. For instance, a disruptive student might be asked to apologize or make amends.

Children with ODD may need adjustments to their learning environment besides behavioral accommodations. This could entail preferential seating near the educator to reduce distractions or using noise-canceling headphones to aid concentration. Establishing structured schedules and routines can also provide stability, which is advantageous for children with ODD. Collaboration between parents and educators is vital in supporting students with ODD. Frequent communication can help identify potential triggers and develop effective strategies to address them. Schools might also consider offering parent-training programs to guide them in managing ODD at home.

Integrating social aptitude development into a young one's learning journey can be priceless, providing them with vital skills to maneuver social encounters skillfully. Such training may involve lessons on efficient communication, empathic understanding, and conflict resolution capabilities.

Lastly, guaranteeing that educators and personnel acquire suitable training in recognizing and addressing ODD is essential. This contributes to creating a compassionate and supportive atmosphere, which nurtures success for every student, encompassing those challenged by ODD.

School support and accommodations for children with ODD are imperative to nurture their academic and social development. Educators can establish a nurturing environment where students with ODD can flourish by creating individualized plans, enforcing clear expectations and consequences, and promoting collaboration between home and school.

EMBRACING THE 7-STEP PLAN FOR PEACE

1. Which part of the 7-step harmony plan struck a chord with you, and how do you intend to integrate it into everyday interactions with your child?
2. Remember when you reacted to your child's negative behavior with irritation or annoyance. What alternative approach could you have taken to apply the 7-step harmony plan and tackle the behavior in a more productive way?
3. What relaxation methods have you introduced to your child thus far, and which ones have been the

most effective in calming and regulating their emotions?

4. Have you involved your child in choosing consequences for their negative behavior? How can you start incorporating their input into the disciplinary process if not?

5. Consider your self-care routine. Are you dedicating enough time to activities you enjoy, and what steps could you take to prioritize self-care in your busy schedule?

6. How can you involve other relatives or caregivers in managing your child's behavior? How can you guarantee uniformity among all the adults in your child's life?

7. Reflect on an instance when your child expressed their emotions or thoughts in a secure and supportive setting. How did you react, and how can you consistently promote open communication with your child?

8. What is your singular goal for your child's behavior management in the upcoming month, and what actions can you undertake to progress toward that objective using the 7-step harmony plan?

STORY

Maintaining a calm household was no easy feat, and Emily and Ethan faced their fair share of challenges. Sometimes, they backslid on their progress, but Emily was determined to keep trying. She delved into various techniques to stay calm herself, recognizing the importance of leading by example. She meticulously created routines and structure for their home, providing a sense of stability that Ethan needed.

As Emily peeled away the layers of frustration, she became adept at identifying Ethan's triggers and implementing effective calming strategies. Their journey was a family affair, with everyone engaging in mindfulness techniques to foster a calmer environment.

However, it wasn't always smooth sailing. Emily's husband often did not see eye to eye with the methods, causing confusion and inconsistency in managing Ethan's behavior. This discord in parenting approaches added another layer of complexity to an already challenging situation.

Through their collective efforts, Emily and Ethan learned that staying calm, even in the face of adversity, was key to navigating the storm of ODD. They developed quick fixes and mindfulness routines that defused tense situations, offering both of them a sense of control and hope for a brighter future.

INTERACTIVE ELEMENT

If you are a parent or caregiver of a child managing ODD, spotting teachable moments to help them acquire constructive habits and coping mechanisms can be beneficial. The suggestions below may aid in compiling a list of such moments.

- **Analyze your child's behavior patterns:** Observe when their conduct becomes especially challenging and strive to identify potential triggers, such as stress, anxiety, fatigue, hunger, or other factors.
- **Pinpoint positive actions to reinforce:** Once triggers are recognized, determine which positive behaviors you want to cultivate in your child. For example, if stress incites acting out, focus on teaching calming techniques like deep breathing or mindfulness. Devise a plan for teaching desired behaviors, employing methods like role-playing, practicing in low-stress situations, or using positive reinforcement to encourage your child to learn new skills.
- **Communicate with your child:** Express your faith in their capacity for positive change and discuss which behaviors to reinforce. Be specific about desired behaviors and shower them with praise and encouragement when they exhibit them.
- **Model positive behavior:** Children learn by observing. This might involve coping strategies during anxious moments or demonstrating effective communication with others.
- **Promote open communication:** Urge your child to share their feelings and concerns while actively

listening. This helps your child feel heard and validated while allowing you to spot potential triggers or areas needing extra support.

- **Celebrate victories:** Acknowledge your child's positive behaviors with verbal praise, a small reward, or a special shared activity. This reinforces good behavior and bolsters their confidence and self-esteem.

Here's a summary of the 7-step plan's key points, in no specific order:

1. Acknowledge and react to your child's positive behavior.
2. Help your child identify their emotions and feelings.
3. Teach coping strategies and critical thinking skills to your child.
4. Establish clear boundaries and rules, and follow through with consequences.
5. Use positive reinforcement and praise to motivate good behavior.
6. Foster a positive, respectful relationship with your child.
7. Seek professional help if required.

THE IMPORTANCE OF KEEPING A CALM ENVIRONMENT

To preserve a delightful home, a peaceful and tranquil atmosphere is vital. Both adults and children can be negatively affected by a chaotic and tense home environment. One way to encourage serenity is through adept communication methods.

It's important for family members to feel free to express their emotions and ideas without fearing judgment or criticism. This open communication fosters a harmonious environment, preventing conflicts and misunderstandings that might otherwise result in stress and tension.

Setting up schedules and routines is another way to sustain a peaceful atmosphere. Establishing specific meal times, homework, and chores helps the family feel more organized and secure. Knowing what to anticipate lessens stress and anxiety, making it simpler to unwind and appreciate each other's presence.

A tidy and organized home also promotes a more serene environment. Clutter and mess can create distracting, bothersome visual noise. Encouraging family members to take responsibility for their belongings and contribute to household tasks helps keep the home neat and orderly.

It is also vital to set limits and boundaries. This involves being clear about acceptable and unacceptable behavior.

Enforcing rules and the consequences for breaking them creates a sense of order and discipline, leading to a calmer home atmosphere.

In summary, maintaining a happy home requires calming the environment. Families can cultivate a serene, harmonious atmosphere that fosters well-being and happiness by adopting effective communication techniques, creating routines, keeping a clean house, and setting limits.

A WELCOME BREAK

Optimism is the faith that leads to achievement. Nothing can be done without hope and confidence.

— HELEN KELLER

Dear Parents,

As you navigate "Defusing Oppositional Defiant Disorder," I want to acknowledge your unwavering commitment to helping your child with ODD. In the midst of your journey, right here in the heart of this book, I want to take a moment with you—a moment to reflect on the dedication and effort you're putting into understanding and supporting your child.

Throughout the chapters leading up to this point, we've explored essential aspects of parenting a child with ODD. Together, we've equipped you with insights and strategies to tackle ODD's challenges. Now, I invite you to take another moment—to recognize the extra steps you've taken to support your child and your growth as a parent. Your journey might still be in progress, but your commitment to understanding and addressing ODD is commendable.

If you'd like to extend this pause for a bit longer, I have a wonderful opportunity for you to assist other parents facing similar challenges. By leaving a review of "Defusing

Oppositional Defiant Disorder" on Amazon, you can guide parents who are seeking help with ODD. Share your experiences and the valuable insights you've gained from this book. Your review will serve as a guiding light for other readers, ensuring they find the assistance they need.

Your dedication to your child's well-being is deeply appreciated, and I am honored to be part of your journey. I encourage you to consider leaving a review to support fellow parents who are on this path with you.

Scan the QR codes to leave a review!

In the United States

In the United Kingdom

A CALMER HOUSE

Right now, I am trying to be in a place of calm, a place where I can chill out and then handle the chaos of life better. You don't just get it overnight; you must work at it.

— JACKEE HARRY

Are you seeking relief from the perpetual chaos and stress in your home? Are you yearning for a serene, harmonious space where your family can thrive? If yes, this chapter is a treasure trove for you. Learn how to identify and address triggers and trouble spots to turn your home into a haven that cultivates positivity, tranquility, and happiness. Dive into this chapter to uncover the pivotal insights on crafting a peaceful home environment where everyone can savor their time together.

HOW TO STAY CALM YOURSELF

Navigating the moment with an ODD child, aiming to prevent major conflicts, requires a unique set of strategies. Here's a collection of essential steps to help you maintain composure and defuse potential blow-ups:

- **Strategic Retreat:** When you sense escalating tension, consider temporarily stepping away. This can prevent immediate conflicts from spiraling further. Take a brief pause to gather your thoughts and emotions. This does not mean to abandon your child. It is okay to tell your child you need a moment but never make them feel you are running away from them.
- **Practice Deep Breathing:** Incorporate deep breathing exercises into your response toolkit. This simple yet effective technique can help you stay grounded and composed when faced with challenging behavior.
- **Stay Calm and Collected:** Make an intentional effort to remain calm and collected, regardless of your child's behavior. This sends a powerful message that you are in control and not easily rattled.

- **Active Listening:** Pay close attention to your child's perspective and feelings. Encourage them to express themselves while you actively listen without interrupting or passing judgment. Sometimes, all they need is to be heard.
- **Avoid Power Struggles:** Choose your battles wisely. Whenever possible, avoid engaging in power struggles that can escalate tensions. Be flexible in your approach and prioritize the overall goal of maintaining peace.
- **Redirect Negative Energy:** Channel your child's negative energy into more positive outlets. Suggest alternative activities or interests that can help shift their focus away from conflict.
- **Offer Choices:** Provide your child with choices within reasonable boundaries. This can empower them to feel more in control and less resistant to your directives.
- **Use Humor:** In appropriate situations, humor can be a valuable tool to defuse tension. A well-timed joke or light-hearted comment can break the cycle of conflict.
- **Positive Reinforcement:** Acknowledge and reward good behavior promptly. Positive reinforcement can motivate your child to engage in positive actions rather than negative ones.
- **Seek Professional Help:** If situations consistently escalate, consider seeking the guidance of a mental

health professional. They can provide valuable insights and strategies tailored to your child's needs.

These steps aim to de-escalate tense moments, reduce the likelihood of a major blow-up, and help maintain a more harmonious environment for you and your child.

CREATE ROUTINES AND STRUCTURE FOR THE HOME

When dealing with ODD, setting up routines and structure in the home can make a significant difference for the entire family. Morning and bedtime routines are especially advantageous, as they offer stability and allow children with ODD to mentally gear up for the day and relax as night approaches. For additional inventive ideas on morning and nighttime routines to benefit children with ODD, explore the "Oppositional Defiant Disorder Workbook."

Incorporating calming activities into morning and bedtime routines can help set the tone for the day and promote relaxation in the evening. For instance, during the morning, a child with ODD could engage in light stretches or breathing exercises before getting dressed and starting their day. This practice can help alleviate stress and anxiety, making facing the day's challenges easier.

Make it a daily ritual to express your love and support for your child before they head out for the day. Share a heartfelt

"I love you" and offer a hug or a high-five to create a positive and affirming atmosphere. Additionally, establish a morning rule that there will be no arguing or conflicts before your child leaves for the day, ensuring a peaceful start.

At night, bedtime routines can include activities that encourage relaxation and signal that it's time to wind down. Reading a book together, listening to calming music, or practicing mindfulness exercises can all contribute to a peaceful bedtime atmosphere. These routines can also serve as an opportunity to reconnect and bond with the child, strengthening the caregiver-child relationship.

Consistent meals, homework, and playtime schedules can further enhance the home environment for children with ODD. These routines foster a sense of stability and help children understand what is expected of them throughout the day. For instance, designating specific times for homework completion and ensuring that playtime follows can create a balanced routine that meets the child's needs for structure and leisure.

Parents and guardians need to maintain consistency when enforcing routines and managing behavior. Following through with consequences for misbehavior and rewarding positive actions can help build trust between the child and caregiver, reducing the frequency of defiant behavior.

In all, establishing morning and bedtime routines can be particularly beneficial for children with ODD, providing a sense of predictability and the opportunity to mentally prepare for the day and unwind at night. Coupled with consistent schedules and clear expectations, these routines can create a supportive and structured home environment, fostering harmony and well-being for the entire family.

PEEL THE ONION

Peeling an onion is a metaphor for examining various aspects of a situation or problem to identify its root causes. When addressing ODD behaviors, "peeling the onion" may involve considering physical factors impacting a child's resilience and mood.

Hunger, poor diet, fatigue, inactivity, illness, pain, dehydration, and gut health can affect a child's behavior and emotional regulation. It is crucial to address these underlying needs, teach your child to recognize their bodily requirements, and encourage them to ask for help when necessary.

Lack of sleep can significantly impact a child's behavior and emotional balance, a vital aspect of physical health. Kids' physical and mental health relies on obtaining adequate sleep. Parents can employ different tactics to aid their children in improving sleep quality.

A crucial approach is to create a consistent sleep routine, including a regular bedtime and wake-up time, along with calming activities before sleep, like reading or taking a warm bath. Creating a sleep-conducive environment is also important. This includes keeping the bedroom dark, quiet, and cool and minimizing electronic device use in the bedroom.

Pay close attention to how your child reacts to different foods. Some children with ODD may be sensitive to particular ingredients or additives that can affect their energy levels and mood. Consider adapting their diet to better suit their needs, as diet can play a role in managing ODD. Additionally, prioritize regular exercise as it can support physical and mental well-being, potentially influencing your child's behavior positively.

Exercise aids in reducing stress and anxiety, enhancing mood, and promoting better sleep. By taking into account these physical aspects and promoting better sleep, a nutritious diet, and consistent exercise, parents can assist their children in managing ODD symptoms and enhancing their overall well-being.

KNOW YOUR CHILD'S TRIGGERS (AND YOURS)

Recognizing your child's and your triggers is a pivotal aspect of effectively managing ODD behavior. These triggers are the specific things, situations, or stimuli that have the potential to evoke anger, frustration, or aggression in your child. Identifying these triggers empowers you to proactively anticipate and address them, either through avoidance strategies or the development of effective coping mechanisms.

It is essential to closely observe your child's behavior and look for patterns to locate triggers. Keep track of any instances in which your child exhibits hostility or agitation and any triggering circumstances or occurrences. For instance, does your child typically become agitated when asked to complete a certain task or when their routine is disrupted? When they feel judged or misunderstood, does your child show defiance?

Being aware of your triggers is also critical as a parent or caregiver. ODD behavior can be difficult and frustrating to deal with, and it's easy to get triggered. Consider developing coping mechanisms to assist you in controlling your emotions in situations that tend to cause you to feel frustrated or angry. Take note of those instances.

Identifying triggers is the first step; subsequently, you can focus on developing strategies to minimize, avoid, or address them when they arise. For instance, if your child becomes upset when given a specific task, consider breaking it down into smaller steps or offering a reward upon completion. If defiance surfaces when the child feels criticized, try employing more positive language and providing praise and encouragement for good behavior.

It is crucial to understand that recognizing triggers and creating strategies to handle them is a continuous process.

What proves effective for one child or situation may not be successful for another, and new triggers may emerge over time. However, with patience, perseverance, and adaptability, you can support your child in managing their triggers and reducing the likelihood of ODD behavior.

HAVE CALMING QUICK FIXES READY

Here are some soothing, quick solutions that might be useful for children and teens.

1. **Relaxation zones:** Create a specific spot within the home where your child can unwind. Fill it with items that aid relaxation, like soft blankets, comfy pillows, or stress balls.
2. **Water therapy:** A bath, shower, or swimming session can help your child relax and rejuvenate.
3. **Song & dance:** Urge your child to sing and dance to their favorite tunes, helping release pent-up energy and reduce stress.
4. **Exercise:** Physical activity can release endorphins and alleviate stress. Suggest a short walk, bike ride, or yoga session.
5. **Art therapy:** Art therapy can help children express emotions and reduce stress. Provide art supplies and encourage creativity.

6. **Sensory play:** Some children find sensory play calming. Offer materials such as sand, water, or playdough.

7. **Deep breathing:** Teach your child to take slow, deep breaths to calm down, useful anytime, anywhere.

8. **Guided meditation:** Use guided meditation apps or videos to help your child relax and release stress.

9. **Aromatherapy:** Calming scents like lavender or vanilla can relax children. Use essential oils or candles to set a soothing ambiance.

10. **Read a book:** Reading helps children focus and forget stressors.

11. **Take a break:** Encourage breaks from tasks if your child feels overwhelmed or frustrated.

12. **Fidget toys:** Fidget toys can be helpful for children who need to occupy their hands.

13. **Music:** Calming music can help your child relax and decompress.

14. **Pet play:** Playing with a pet can reduce stress and elevate mood.

15. **Stress balls:** Stress balls help release tension and alleviate stress.

16. **Weighted blanket:** Weighted blankets can provide comfort and security for some children.

17. **Progressive muscle relaxation:** Tensing and relaxing specific muscle groups can reduce tension and stress.

18. **Mindful walks:** Encourage your child to walk and observe their surroundings, noticing sights, sounds, and sensations.

19. **Positive affirmations:** Encourage your child to repeat positive affirmations, like "I am calm and in control."

TEACH YOUR WHOLE FAMILY MINDFULNESS TECHNIQUES

Introducing mindfulness practices to your family may benefit children with ODD and everyone else in the household. These approaches can help alleviate stress and anxiety, sharpen focus and attention, and boost happiness. Here are some approaches to impart mindfulness to those dear to you.

- Mindful breathing: Encourage your kin to be conscious of their breath, drawing in and releasing deep, unhurried breaths. This straightforward technique can soothe the mind and body with ease.
- Mindful appreciation: Encourage your family to dedicate daily moments to reflect on what they're grateful for. This practice can cultivate a positive attitude and increase joy and satisfaction.
- Mindful eating: Prompt your family to eat leisurely, savoring the flavors, scents, and textures of their meals. This conscious tactic can nudge them to be

more aware of their feeding patterns, steering them toward healthier options.

- Mindful motion: Urge your loved ones to dabble in yoga, tai chi, or other mindful movements. These endeavors can aid in stress relief and boost bodily well-being.

- Mindful listening: Urge your family to be aware of the sounds surrounding them, whether it's the melody of birdsong or the hum of traffic. This practice can heighten awareness of the present moment and foster relaxation.

- Mindful walking: Encourage your family to stroll, paying attention to each step's sensation. This enjoyable activity can help decrease stress and boost physical exercise.

- Mindful visualization: Inspire your family to envision a tranquil and soothing scene, like a beach or a forest. This practice can help ease stress and encourage relaxation.

By integrating these mindfulness practices into your daily life, you can assist everyone in your family to feel more peaceful, centered, and composed.

PARENTING STYLES AND ODD

Navigating the complex world of parenting is an immense undertaking, especially for those with children diagnosed with ODD. How a parent raises their child can significantly influence the child's growth, behavior, and management of ODD symptoms. Considering this, let's delve into various parenting styles and how they impact children with ODD.

Characterized by stringent rules and lofty expectations with minimal warmth or nurturing, authoritarian parenting adheres to a "my way or the highway" mindset, insisting on unwavering obedience from children. When applied to ODD, this parenting approach may aggravate a child's defiance and result in heightened power struggles. Feeling trapped, children may react with increased aggression, hindering the parent and the child from resolving conflicts constructively.

Conversely, permissive parenting involves abundant warmth and affection but sparse boundaries or expectations. Parents following this style tend to prioritize their child's happiness and may avoid establishing limits to avert confrontation. However, the absence of structure and guidance might worsen behavioral issues for children with ODD. They could struggle with self-regulation, impulse control, and cultivating a sense of accountability for their actions.

Finding equilibrium between the rigidness of authoritarian parenting and the permissiveness of indulgent parenting, authoritative parenting is frequently heralded as the optimal approach. This method incorporates clear expectations and boundaries, complemented by open communication, warmth, and empathy. Parents who practice authoritative parenting seek to nurture autonomy and responsibility in their children, addressing their emotional needs and providing guidance through challenges.

Apart from these main parenting styles, there is an increasing interest in more specialized strategies tailored to address the distinct challenges confronted by children with ODD. Techniques such as collaborative and proactive solutions (CPS) and parent management training (PMT) underscore the value of collaboration, empathy, and problem-solving skills, enabling parents and children to discover mutually beneficial resolutions.

Ultimately, pinpointing the most effective parenting style for a child with ODD is a highly personalized process. Parents must consider the unique needs, disposition, and intensity of their child's symptoms when selecting the best-suited method for their family situation. Irrespective of the selected style, the crux is to stay adaptable, empathetic, and patient, as handling ODD often demands a long-term and ongoing commitment.

BUILDING A SUPPORTIVE ENVIRONMENT REFLECTION

- What do you think triggers your child's behavior? How can you minimize or eradicate those catalysts going forward?

- What instant calming techniques have you experimented with for your child?
- Have you established structure and routine within your household? If so, did you make the routines visible and involve your child?
- What enjoyable family traditions have you incorporated into your daily life? How have they boosted your child's sense of enthusiasm and involvement?
- How have you educated your child to recognize and ask for help with their physical needs?
- Have you refined self-care practices as a family unit?
- What approaches have you employed to stay composed while addressing your child's ODD conduct? Have they been effective?
- Have you recognized your child's achievements in following routines and applying calming techniques? How have you offered positive reinforcement?
- Have you been consistent in outlining and adhering to schedules? If not, what measures can you take to become more reliable?
- How do you plan to persist in diminishing triggers, setting up routines, and fostering mindfulness within your family moving forward?

ALTERNATIVE AND COMPLEMENTARY THERAPIES FOR ODD

While seeking effective ways to address ODD, it is crucial to consider alternative and complementary therapies. These unconventional techniques can offer additional support to children with ODD and their families alongside more traditional treatments like medication and behavioral therapy.

Art therapy is an innovative method worth exploring. This approach enables children struggling with ODD to express their emotions and thoughts in a secure, non-aggressive setting using various artistic mediums, such as drawing, painting, or sculpting. Children can gain deeper insight into their feelings and actions by externalizing their emotions. Art therapy can also nurture a sense of accomplishment and self-esteem, empowering children with ODD to develop positive coping mechanisms and build healthier relationships with others.

Another promising option is equine therapy, which involves interacting with horses to encourage emotional growth and learning. This technique is particularly valuable for young people with ODD, as it promotes responsibility for their actions, enhances communication skills, and fosters empathy. Engaging with these gentle creatures can teach essential life skills like patience, trust, and cooperation, which are often challenging for individuals with ODD to master.

Furthermore, equine therapy can alleviate anxiety and improve overall emotional well-being.

Integrating mindfulness practices, as mentioned earlier, can also benefit ODD management. Consistent mindfulness practice can teach these children to respond to their emotions more effectively, reducing the intensity and frequency of outbursts and defiance.

Instead of replacing established approaches such as medication and behavioral therapy, alternative therapies should augment these evidence-based methods, forging a holistic and customized care plan to suit the child's requirements.

BENEFITS AND LIMITATIONS OF THESE THERAPIES

Alternative treatments for ODD can provide essential aid and resources to children and their families while supplementing conventional interventions such as medication and behavioral therapy. Nevertheless, assessing the advantages and drawbacks of these methods is vital to guarantee they suit a child's distinct needs and situation.

A key advantage of alternative treatments is their capacity to deliver a comprehensive approach to ODD management. Methods like art therapy, equine therapy, and mindfulness practices address multiple facets of a child's well-being, encompassing emotional, social, and cognitive development. By targeting these aspects, alternative treatments can assist children with ODD in acquiring healthier coping strategies, enhancing their self-awareness, and fostering improved communication skills.

Another benefit of alternative treatments is their potential to involve children in a non-intimidating and nurturing environment. Numerous children with ODD might be resistant to conventional therapy settings, complicating the establishment of trust and progress. Alternative treatments can present a more engaging and less adversarial environment, potentially inspiring children to be more open to the therapeutic process.

Moreover, alternative treatments can be customized to a child's preferences and strengths, fostering achievement and self-esteem. When children are engaged and triumphant in their therapeutic activities, they are more inclined to stay motivated to tackle their challenges inside and outside the therapy setting.

Despite these advantages, some drawbacks must be considered when integrating alternative treatments into a child's ODD treatment plan. One notable drawback is the insufficient research and scientific evidence supporting the efficacy of some alternative treatments. While numerous personal accounts underscore the success of these methods, more thorough studies are required to ascertain their overall effectiveness in treating ODD.

An additional drawback is that alternative treatments could be time-consuming and expensive. Certain therapies might necessitate significant time and resources, and families may have to consider the advantages against the financial and logistical obstacles of pursuing these treatments. Furthermore, finding qualified professionals specializing in particular alternative treatments could be challenging, restricting access to these resources for some families.

It is essential to emphasize that alternative treatments must not be used as substitutes for evidence-based interventions like medication and behavioral therapy. Although unconventional methods can be valuable components of a child's treatment plan, they should be used alongside traditional therapies to optimize their effectiveness.

INTERACTIVE ELEMENT

Here's a compilation of 50 calming activities for children across various age groups.

For younger children (ages 3–6):

- Breathe deeply together.
- Read a beloved story.
- Engage with Play-Doh or clay.
- Offer a warm embrace.
- Look through family photos.
- Play gentle music.

- Color or draw in a picture book.
- Play with a sensory bin or sensory bottle.
- Blow bubbles.
- Take a nature walk and search for bugs.

For children (ages 7–12):

- Practice deep breathing techniques.
- Maintain a journal.
- Try guided meditation or visualization.
- Do yoga or stretches together.
- Play board games.
- Assemble a puzzle.
- Host a dance party.
- Use stress balls or fidget toys.
- Engage in a calming game, such as solitaire or Go Fish.

For teenagers (ages 13–18):

- Indulge in a long, warm shower or bath.
- Keep a gratitude journal.
- Solve crossword or Sudoku puzzles.
- Play soothing music
- Practice mindful meditation.
- Craft a homemade project.
- Sing or play a musical instrument.
- Exercise or go for a run.

- Explore progressive muscle relaxation.

For all ages:

- Take a break from screens.
- Embrace the outdoors and nature.
- Step away from social media.
- Stretch or engage in light exercise.
- Practice positive affirmations.
- Experience guided visualization.
- Enjoy a quiet moment of reflection.
- Spend quality time with a pet.
- Give yourself a massage or foot rub.
- Drink water or herbal tea.
- Try aromatherapy with essential oils.
- Jot down daily gratitude lists or notes.
- Use a weighted blanket or cuddle a stuffed animal.
- Listen to a relaxing podcast or audiobook.
- Perform a brain dump to express thoughts and worries.
- Play a card or board game.
- Pause multitasking.
- Use a stress ball or squeeze toy.
- Apply a hot or cold pack.
- Develop visualization or imagery skills.

STORY

Emily's efforts to maintain a calm household resonate with the importance of managing triggers and promoting mindfulness, as discussed in this chapter. These techniques are instrumental in defusing tense situations. While initially, there were differences in parenting approaches between Emily and her husband, with time and concerted effort, they started to work together. They both realized that being on the same page made for a significantly calmer environment for Ethan. This united front offered him the consistency and support he needed as he grappled with ODD. Things were certainly better but more help and intervention was still needed.

WHAT ARE YOUR OTHER ODD TREATMENT OPTIONS?

Tackling ODD is intricate, but various treatment choices are available for children and teens facing this tough condition. Parents can explore other ODD treatment options in partnership with mental health professionals beyond merely employing positive behavior techniques and soothing methods at home and school.

CBT (Cognitive Behavioral Therapy) is a popular approach for addressing ODD, assisting children in cultivating new coping methods and altering their viewpoints on their actions and feelings. CBT can be conducted one-on-one or within group environments, often combined with additional treatments like medication.

Medicinal solutions can be valuable in managing ODD, especially when accompanied by other mental health issues like ADHD or anxiety. Various medicines, such as mood balancers, stimulants, and antidepressants, might be proposed to help lessen the manifestations of ODD. Check out my book Parenting a Child with ADHD for more indepth insights into ADHD behaviors and traits.

Family therapy is another effective option for addressing ODD, as it assists parents and siblings in grasping and adapting to the difficulties associated with this disorder. It fosters better communication, promotes positive interactions, and diminishes family conflicts.

Moreover, parent training programs can prove advantageous for families with ODD-affected children. These programs frequently instruct parents on new approaches to handling their child's behavior while enhancing their connection with their offspring.

Parents must collaborate closely with mental health professionals to pinpoint the most appropriate ODD treatment options tailored to their child's needs and situation. Children with ODD can learn to control their symptoms and flourish with the proper assistance and treatment.

TIPS FOR FINDING QUALIFIED PROFESSIONALS

Undertaking the mission to find highly skilled experts for children diagnosed with ODD is a crucial step in their therapeutic journey. Connecting with the right professionals can provide invaluable guidance and customized strategies and profoundly impact your family's well-being and child's life.

Embarking on this search, a fabulous place to start is with your child's pediatrician or primary care physician. These individuals often possess a wealth of expertise in identifying professionals with specific proficiencies related to ODD.

It is essential to delve into the credentials of potential professionals, focusing on their academic qualifications, certifications, and licenses. Remember that the qualifications can vary greatly, so seeking someone who thoroughly comprehends ODD is crucial.

The counsel of other parents who have navigated the same waters can offer invaluable input on locating the right professionals. Support groups, both online and in person, can act as treasure troves of information, with parents eager to recommend professionals they've had positive experiences with.

Don't underestimate the potency of reputable online directories and professional organizations. These can serve as effective avenues for discovering qualified ODD experts in your vicinity.

Before you commit to a professional, schedule an initial meeting to gauge if their communication approach aligns with your preferences. Finding someone who can develop a customized plan tailored to your child's specific needs and circumstances is important.

Cultural considerations and language preferences can play a significant role in fostering a successful therapeutic relationship. Be sure to evaluate whether the professional's background and language abilities align with your requirements.

Practical elements like location, office hours, and accessibility should be considered. A professional with a convenient office and availability could prove instrumental in successfully treating your child.

To sum up, taking the plunge to find qualified professionals for your ODD-affected child is a vital component of their treatment and well-being. By considering the abovementioned factors, conducting comprehensive research, and exercising patience and determination, you will find the right expert to support your child and your family on this challenging journey.

OTHER OPTIONS

Health is a complete harmony of the body, mind, and spirit.
When one is free from physical disabilities and mental
distractions, the soul's gates open.

— B. K. S. IYENGAR

By now, you might be feeling exhausted by the limited
therapy options available for ODD. It is time to look
beyond conventional methods and explore alternative or
more natural possibilities that could benefit your child. This
chapter will examine various opportunities that may offer
new hope for treating your child's ODD. It is worth noting
that about 67% of children with ODD who undergo treat-

ment experience symptom relief within three years (Thompson, 2021).

ODD is a complex and demanding condition, typically necessitating a comprehensive approach combining various therapies and behavior management techniques.

MEDICATION

When discussing mental health, the topic of medication for ODD piques curiosity and sparks contemplation. The human psyche, a tapestry woven with convoluted intricacies, fortitude, and susceptibility, has eternally captured the imagination of curious minds. The necessity for medication in managing ODD is shrouded in debate; however, one cannot dismiss the indelible influence these interventions may bestow upon those grappling with this enigmatic affliction.

As mentioned earlier, ODD is characterized by a persistent pattern of defiant, disobedient, and hostile behavior toward authority figures. This behavioral disorder affects children and adolescents, often causing distress and disrupting the harmonious balance within families, schools, and communities. Medication may be considered an option in certain cases in the quest for effective treatment.

Medications for ODD are not typically a first-line treatment, as the condition is often best managed through behavioral therapies, parental training, and other psychosocial interventions. When ODD is accompanied by conditions like

ADHD or anxiety, the prescription of medication may serve as a beacon of relief for the struggling individual. Embarking on the journey of pharmacological intervention, one inadvertently discovers stimulant medications like Ritalin and Adderall, frequently used to confront the manifestations of ADHD. These elixirs have the potential to alleviate select ODD behaviors when ADHD presents itself as an intertwined condition.

Similarly, non-stimulant medications, such as Strattera and Intuniv, can be summoned for their propitious impact on reining in impulsiveness and tempering aggression.

When anxiety becomes intertwined with a condition, individuals may find relief through selective serotonin reuptake inhibitors (SSRIs) like Prozac and Zoloft. These medications, designed to regulate mood and alleviate anxiety, could help reduce behavioral symptoms associated with the condition.

Each individual, with a unique constellation of experiences and chemistry, requires a tailored approach to navigate the labyrinth of ODD and its treatment. The journey through the woods of pharmaceutical intervention is laden with potential side effects and individual responses that must be carefully considered. As we tread this path, it is crucial to consult with a qualified mental health professional, ensuring the most appropriate and effective treatment is tailored to each unique individual navigating the murky waters of ODD.

THERAPY-BASED OPTIONS

Embarking upon exploring therapy-based options for ODD, we find ourselves amidst various fascinating approaches, each with unique merits. The essence of therapy lies in empowering individuals to develop coping strategies and hone their personal and social functioning. Let me unravel the tapestry of such therapeutic options, weaving a narrative that captures the essence of these wondrous methods.

CBT focuses on transforming negative thought patterns and behaviors, presenting a goal-oriented and structured path for individuals to tread. Through CBT, people can learn to identify and restructure their negative beliefs and viewpoints, ultimately acquiring more effective ways to cope with life's challenges. ODD, with its defiant and hostile demeanor toward authority figures, finds itself particularly susceptible to the transformative power of CBT.

A pivotal element of CBT's effectiveness in treating ODD is its ability to equip individuals with new coping skills, problem-solving techniques, and enhanced social abilities. CBT helps individuals with ODD replace negative thoughts with a neutral or positive outlook by teaching them to engage with others more constructively and positively. Studies, such as the one conducted by Eyberg and colleagues (2008), provide tangible evidence of CBT's efficacy in alleviating ODD symptoms and improving child and family functioning.

Parent-child interaction therapy (PCIT) offers another intriguing avenue for intervention. This short-term, evidence-based approach focuses on enhancing the quality of the parent-child relationship and diminishing destructive behavioral patterns in children. PCIT, originally designed for children between two and seven years old with disruptive behavior disorders like ODD, has since evolved to accommodate older children and those with diverse diagnoses.

The crux of PCIT lies in teaching parents new skills to foster a more positive and effective connection with their children. Therapists guide parents in real-time interactions with their children, providing feedback and helping them adopt tailored parenting techniques suited to the child's specific needs. The therapeutic odyssey unfolds in two distinct phases—child-directed interaction (CDI) and parent-directed interaction (PDI). Child-led play flourishes in the CDI sphere in this intricate dance, while the PDI domain embraces the art of parent-guided engagements.

Social skills training, a therapy that emphasizes fostering positive social skills and communication techniques, offers promising results for those grappling with ODD. Social skills training can reduce conflicts and improve overall functioning by enabling individuals to develop more confident and effective ways of connecting with others. This form of therapy often involves role-playing, modeling, and feedback to help individuals refine their interactions with others.

Play therapy, an artful incarnation of psychotherapy tailored for young souls, bestows a sanctuary for tender beings grappling with personal, behavioral, or psychological tribulations, enabling them to unfurl their emotions and sentiments in a nurturing environment. This creative form of therapy incorporates art therapy, sand play therapy, and puppet therapy, among others. In the context of ODD, play therapy can help children learn new coping strategies and cultivate positive methods of communication.

For children with ODD, play therapy operates on the principle of allowing them to take the lead during sessions. The therapist provides assistance and direction when necessary, nurturing a growing connection of trust and rapport between themselves and the child. Play therapy can significantly contribute to the development of positive coping mechanisms and emotional regulation by providing a secure and supportive environment for children to express their thoughts.

In conclusion, many therapy-based options exist for addressing ODD, each boasting its unique strengths. CBT, PCIT, social-skills training, and play therapy are a few of the diverse therapeutic approaches that can help individuals with ODD learn new coping skills, enhance their problem-solving techniques, and improve their interpersonal abilities. By exploring these therapeutic options, we take a step closer to understanding the captivating landscape of ODD treatment.

SUPPLEMENTATION OPTIONS

Alternative options, such as supplements, might enhance the management of ODD symptoms alongside conventional treatments. Omega-3 fatty acids, probiotics, and magnesium stand out as supplements that have been examined for their capacity to mitigate ODD symptoms. Omega-3 fatty acids hold a key position in fostering brain growth and function. Several studies suggest that omega-3 supplements could reduce ODD manifestations like impulsivity, hyperactivity, and antagonism (Papadopoulos, 2018). Omega-3 can be obtained from fish like salmon, mackerel, and sardines or supplements. Nevertheless, it is vital to recognize that the research on omega-3 supplements' effectiveness for ODD remains limited, and further studies are necessary.

Live microorganisms called probiotics, famous for promoting gut wellness and bolstering immunity, might also offer advantages for one's psychological well-being. They may potentially reduce symptoms of anxiety and depression. Given the frequent association of anxiety and mood disorders with ODD, probiotics might be valuable in managing ODD symptoms. Probiotics can be discovered in items such as yogurt, kefir, and supplements.

Some evidence suggests that magnesium supplements could help decrease anxiety symptoms and elevate overall mood (Health Match staff, 2022). Excellent sources of magnesium encompass dark leafy greens, nuts, seeds, and supplements.

Nonetheless, as with omega-3 supplements, further investigation is necessary to ascertain the potency of magnesium supplements when tackling ODD symptoms.

It is imperative to emphasize that supplements should not be the primary treatment for ODD. They should instead complement traditional treatments, such as therapy and medication.

To round up, supplement options, including omega-3 fatty acids, probiotics, and magnesium, might aid in managing ODD symptoms. Working closely with a healthcare professional to develop the most suitable treatment plan for each individual is critically important.

NAVIGATING THE HEALTHCARE SYSTEM

The starting point for addressing this concern may not be immediately apparent, but it is crucial to take a moment and embark on this journey for the child's benefit. With determination and perseverance, locating the right assistance is achievable.

Initiate the process by consulting a pediatrician with the necessary expertise to recognize and evaluate ODD. As mentioned repeatedly in this book, engaging a reliable healthcare professional is an indispensable initial move in ascertaining the most suitable course of action.

Upon obtaining a diagnosis, the subsequent stage entails investigating potential treatment methods. These therapeutic techniques have proven effective in addressing ODD symptoms and enhancing the child's overall well-being. Collaborating with teachers and support staff can help develop a comprehensive plan to address ODD-related challenges in the classroom. Integrating input from various sources will create a more complete picture of the child's needs and the best strategies to address them.

Health insurance is often an unavoidable topic in healthcare. Ensure that the insurance plan covers the necessary treatments and interventions for ODD, and if not, explore alternative options. Advocating for the child's needs is vital, even if it entails endless back-and-forth with insurance providers.

Remember to seek assistance from caregivers, too, as raising a child with ODD can be both emotionally and physically draining. Connecting with those facing similar challenges can offer comfort and valuable guidance. The understanding and support of a compassionate community can be incredibly soothing and strengthening.

EXPLORING TREATMENT OPTIONS

1. What do you think and feel about medicine as a treatment choice for ODD? Have your viewpoints about taking drugs changed after reading this chapter?

2. Contemplate the experiences with therapy-oriented options, such as PCIT and social skills training. In what ways have these therapeutic approaches been beneficial for both you and your child?

3. Have you ever considered play therapy as a treatment for your child's ODD side effects? How would play therapy help your child?

4. What are your thoughts on using probiotics as a supplementary option to manage ODD symptoms?

5. Would you consider trying probiotics as a supplement for your child?

6. How do you envision the role of supplements like omega-3 fatty acids in managing ODD symptoms? Have you ever tried incorporating these supplements into your child's diet?

7. Reflect upon your experiences with medication as a treatment for your child's ODD symptoms.

8. How has your child responded to therapy-based options, such as PCIT and social skills training? Have you noticed any changes in their behavior or overall functioning?

9. Have you ever made an effort to boost omega-3 fatty acids in your child's meals to aid in ODD symptom control?

10. What are your thoughts about using magnesium supplements as a possible remedy for ODD manifestations?

11. Has incorporating magnesium in your child's nutritional plan been something you have experimented with before?

12. Think about the overall experiences with various treatment options for your child's ODD symptoms. Which approaches have proven most beneficial up to this point, and what obstacles have arisen during the process?

STORY

Emily and Ethan explore various treatment options, including therapy and medication. This chapter delves into the different modalities available to families dealing with ODD and highlights the importance of individualized treatment plans. Despite their progress in managing ODD, there were still instances when Ethan's explosive behaviors could turn violent, and the challenges of dealing with ODD at school persisted. They often struggled to communicate effectively with teachers, who sometimes misunderstood the nature of ODD. These ongoing hurdles emphasized the need for a comprehensive approach to treatment and support.

SITUATIONAL SOLUTIONS

Between stimulus and response, there is a space. In that space is our power to choose our response. In our response lies our growth and our freedom.

— VIKTOR E. FRANKL

Unraveling the complexities of ODD and the strategies that may assist those engulfed in its clutches is a quest that demands patience and persistence. However, hidden within this storm of emotions, there are situational solutions that may provide a beacon of light to guide those affected toward calmer shores.

These solutions, like the key to a hidden door, are meant to unlock the potential within each unique situation and empower all involved.

Situational solutions for ODD encompass myriad diverse strategies that mandate thoughtful contemplation and tailor-made adjustments to align with the distinctive needs of each individual gracefully. Whether through the implementation of positive reinforcement, the cultivation of emotional regulation skills, or the establishment of clear boundaries and expectations, situational solutions offer a multitude of paths to explore in the pursuit of a more balanced and fulfilling life.

BEHAVIORAL CONTRACTS

A behavioral contract is not some magical, all-encompassing solution, but has its merits. It is like a roadmap, providing a clear path to follow, with specific expectations and consequences outlined.

Imagine this scenario: Parent and child join forces, crafting a contract that explicitly lays out behavior expectations, the corresponding rewards for meeting them, and the consequences for any lapses. Through this collaborative approach, the child gains a crystal-clear understanding of the expectations, leaving no room for confusion or uncertainty.

However, the truly remarkable facet of this contractual arrangement is that it transcends the boundaries of a one-sided, authoritarian dictate imposed by the parent. Quite the opposite, it embodies a collaborative endeavor where both participants actively engage in the crafting process. It is akin to constructing something together, a framework that offers support and guidance to the child as they navigate the challenges of ODD.

A behavioral contract is only as effective as the effort put into it, and it requires regular review and tweaking to ensure it remains relevant and effective. But isn't that like life, constantly evolving, adapting, and growing? A never-ending dance of learning and development?

In the grand scheme, a behavioral contract for ODD might not be the be-all and end-all solution. But it's a start, a stepping stone, a way to provide some semblance of order in ODD's chaos. And sometimes, that is all that's needed—a helping hand to guide you through the tangled web of emotions and challenges that come with ODD. Like finding a patch of sunlight in a dense forest, that little hope and guidance can make all the difference.

However, let us not forget that a behavioral contract is not a one-and-done affair. It requires constant communication, revisiting, and reevaluating. As the child grows and evolves, so too must the contract. It is a living, breathing document, a testament to the ongoing commitment of both parent and child to work together to overcome ODD's challenges.

Imagine the surge of fulfillment and satisfaction from witnessing advancement and development while acknowledging that it is the outcome of a joint effort. The child feels empowered and supported, knowing their parent is by their side, working together toward a common goal. It is like a symphony, a harmonious blending of efforts, culminating in something beautiful.

And who knows? Perhaps the very act of creating and maintaining a behavioral contract could lead to unforeseen benefits. Strengthened bonds, improved communication, and a deeper understanding of one another—all invaluable gifts in their own right. It is like the proverbial cherry on top, the unexpected bonus that makes the whole process even more worthwhile.

So, in the end, while a behavioral contract for ODD might not be a panacea, it does offer a glimmer of hope, a guiding light in the murky waters of managing the condition. It is not perfect, but what in life truly is?

How to Develop Behavioral Contracts

In the "Defusing Oppositional Defiant Disorder Workbook," you will find a comprehensive breakdown of the elements that make up a successful behavioral contract. This invaluable resource guides you through creating a contract that clearly outlines behavior expectations, rewards for meeting those expectations, and consequences for any deviations.

DEFUSING OPPOSITIONAL DEFIANT DISORDER | 153

Developing a behavioral contract can be collaborative between parents, educators, and therapists. Here are some methodical guidelines and suggestions to adhere to.

Step 1: Pinpoint the problematic behavior

The initial stride in creating a behavioral contract begins with the crucial step of identifying the specific behaviors that need attention. Parents should closely observe and monitor their child's actions, understanding which behaviors require modification or improvement.

Open communication with the child is essential to gain insight into their perspective on these behaviors and whether they agree that these actions need adjustment. In addition to discussions with the child, parents can collaborate with teachers, therapists, or other adults who interact with the child. Gathering insights from multiple sources develops a comprehensive understanding of the behavior in question, paving the way for more effective and holistic solutions.

Step 2: Establish expectations

Once the problematic behavior is identified, the next phase outlines the expectations or goals the child should strive to attain. Defining precise, quantifiable, and achievable expectations that the child can comprehend and work toward is essential. The expectations should be age-appropriate and realistic.

To set expectations, parents should involve the child in the process. The child's input and comprehension of the expectations can increase their commitment to attaining the objectives. It is also crucial to keep the expectations straightforward and focused so the child knows their tasks.

One helpful approach for establishing expectations is using the "SMART" criteria. SMART stands for Specific, Measurable, Attainable, Relevant, and Time-bound (Herrity, 2022). Specific expectations unambiguously define the child's tasks. Measurable expectations can be evaluated to track progress. Attainable expectations are sensible and achievable. Relevant expectations align with the overall goal of the behavioral contract. Time-bound expectations have a definite deadline or time frame for completion.

Step 3: Determine rewards

Rewards play a pivotal role in motivating children to improve their conduct. When forming a behavioral contract, it is crucial to pinpoint rewards that matter to the child. Tangible rewards, like toys, games, and other items, can be motivating, but intangible rewards, such as praise, recognition, and accolades, can also be potent. Age-appropriateness is another vital consideration when selecting rewards. Younger children may be motivated by stickers, small toys, or treats, while older children might prefer screen time or more significant rewards, like an allowance increase.

Rewards should also cater to the child's interests. For instance, a child who enjoys video games might be motivated by extra gaming time, while a sports-loving child might be encouraged by game tickets or new sports gear. By selecting rewards that align with the child's interests, parents can increase the child's likelihood of striving for the desired behavior.

Step 4: Decide on consequences

Consequences play a pivotal role within a behavioral contract, serving as a tool to help children understand the potential results of their actions. When formulating consequences, it is crucial to ensure they are fair and proportionate to the specific behavior being addressed.

For instance, a minor infraction, such as failing to complete homework, might warrant a milder consequence, such as temporarily forfeiting a privilege. On the other hand, a more serious transgression, like physical aggression, may necessitate a more substantial repercussion.

Consistency and enforceability are also crucial factors when choosing consequences. It is essential to ensure that consequences can be enforced and are consistently applied to all behaviors. For instance, if a child loses screen time because of incomplete homework, it is crucial to ensure they do not access screen time until they have finished the homework, and the parent must enforce this consequence.

It is also crucial to ensure that consequences are communicated clearly to the child so they understand the potential outcomes of their actions. Parents should convey consequences clearly to the child and ensure they comprehend the connection between their actions and the consequences. This clarity can help the child grasp the relationship between their actions and the outcomes, motivating them to improve their behavior.

Step 5: Draft the contract

Once you have outlined the goals and expectations for the behavioral contract, it is time to document it formally. The agreement must encompass expectations, incentives, and repercussions, in addition to detailing the time frame for the contract. It is of utmost importance to ascertain that all parties involved in the agreement are in harmony, averting any misapprehension regarding anticipated outcomes. Contemplate incorporating precise actions that necessitate modification and communicate how the child can actualize these transformations.

While formulating the contract, remember that it should be customized to cater to the unique child and their specific requirements. It is essential to set realistic expectations and goals that the child can feasibly achieve; otherwise, the contract may become discouraging or even counterproductive. It is also vital to ensure that the rewards and consequences are appropriate for the child's age, interests, and motivation.

Step 6: Sign and review the contract

After the agreement has been meticulously written, the moment has arrived to affix your signatures. The child, parents, and other participating parties should all sign the contract to indicate their agreement with its terms. This step is crucial in establishing accountability and responsibility for the contract.

It is also essential to regularly review the contract to ensure it remains relevant and effective. Depending on the child's progress, you may need to adjust the expectations, rewards, and consequences outlined in the contract. This can be achieved through ongoing communication, feedback with the child, and regular check-ins and updates with other participating parties.

Regularly reviewing the contract also helps keep everyone accountable and motivated. It provides an opportunity to celebrate progress and successes and address any challenges or setbacks that may arise. Additionally, reviewing the contract can help reinforce the child's commitment to the behavioral changes they have agreed to make.

In conclusion, behavioral contracts can effectively promote positive behaviors and discourage negative conduct in children with ODD.

COMMON CHALLENGES ENCOUNTERED BY CHILDREN WITH ODD AND CORRESPONDING SITUATIONAL SOLUTIONS

Common challenges faced by children with Oppositional Defiant Disorder (ODD) can often create significant stress for both the child and their caregivers. While I could offer specific advice for various situations, it's important to remember that the solutions you seek can often be found within the valuable insights you've gathered throughout the book. As you've journeyed through the chapters, the reflection sections have provided a space for you to connect with the material and apply it to your unique circumstances. To address these common challenges effectively, consider revisiting those moments of self-reflection, as the answers and guidance you seek for specific situations can often be discovered there. This approach empowers you as a caregiver and encourages a deeper understanding of how to apply the knowledge gained from this book to the real-life challenges of parenting a child with ODD.

Here are some situations you may encounter. Take a proactive approach to parenting your child with ODD. Document your plan for addressing each challenging situation listed above, ensuring you have a clear strategy in place before these situations arise. Preparedness can empower you to respond effectively and reduce stress in the heat of the moment

- Morning Routine Battles: Difficulty getting the child ready for school or other morning activities.
- Homework Resistance: Struggles with completing homework assignments without defiance.
- Defiance During Shopping: Refusal to follow instructions or causing disruptions in stores.
- Bedtime Resistance: Resistance to bedtime routines and difficulties falling asleep.
- Disruptive Behavior in School: Receiving teacher reports of disruptive or defiant behavior.
- Managing Aggressive Outbursts: Dealing with temper tantrums, physical aggression, or verbal hostility.
- Transitioning Between Tasks: Difficulty moving from one activity or task to another.
- Resistance to Non-Preferred Activities: Unwillingness to engage in activities the child doesn't enjoy.
- Sibling Conflicts: Frequent conflicts and arguments with siblings.
- Social Skills Challenges: Struggles with making friends or maintaining positive relationships.
- Mealtime Battles: Refusal to eat certain foods or engage in mealtime routines.
- Excessive Screen Time: Difficulty managing screen time limits and tantrums when screen time is restricted.

- Refusal to Attend Therapy: Resistance to attending therapy sessions or other recommended interventions.
- Public Meltdowns: Tantrums or meltdowns in public places, leading to embarrassment.
- Noncompliance with Instructions: Ignoring or outright refusal to follow parental or authority figures' instructions.
- Lying: Addressing situations where the child lies about their actions, responsibilities, or compliance with rules and expectations.
- Lack of Accountability: Confronting instances where the child avoids taking responsibility for their actions or mistakes and shifts blame onto others.

These situations can vary in intensity and frequency but are common challenges that parents of children with ODD may encounter. Developing effective strategies for managing these situations is crucial to supporting the child's growth and well-being while reducing stress for both the child and the parents.

JOBS FOR PEOPLE WITH ODD

Exploring the employment landscape might be intimidating for individuals with ODD. You are not wrong to worry that your child may experience some difficulty in finding their place in the workforce. Finding a suitable career that caters to their distinct requirements and abilities can make a difference. Several career options may fit individuals with ODD, provided the work setting and responsibilities align with their aptitudes and inclinations.

One potential career path for people with ODD lies in creative arts, such as writing, illustration, or graphic design. These professions often offer increased flexibility and autonomy, granting a platform for self-expression and a constructive means to channel emotions. Additionally, many creative jobs can be pursued freelance or via remote work arrangements, enabling greater control over one's work environment and schedule.

Entrepreneurship is another area where individuals with ODD might thrive. Starting a business or becoming a self-employed professional can afford the self-reliance and liberty that someone with ODD may find attractive. In this capacity, one can create personal targets, make thoughtful decisions, and be held accountable for their actions without adhering to the usual workplace standards. Still, having a solid support system and access to essential resources is key to addressing the hurdles of being an entrepreneur.

Careers involving critical thinking and problem-solving may also suit those with ODD. Roles in fields like engineering, computer programming, or scientific research can be appropriate, as they often demand high focus, analytical skills, and persistence. These roles tend to be more structured, which can provide a sense of reliability and consistency for individuals with ODD.

Physically demanding or outdoor jobs, such as working with animals, construction, or landscaping, can appeal to people with ODD who enjoy hands-on tasks and prefer to avoid traditional office settings. Doing physically challenging work can also be a healthy outlet for energy and frustration, potentially alleviating ODD symptoms.

It is important to note that the perfect job for someone with ODD depends on their interests, skills, and symptom severity. To boost job satisfaction and success, individuals with ODD should consider seeking workplace accommodations, like flexible scheduling or additional support from coworkers or supervisors. Therapy or support groups can also aid in managing symptoms and developing coping strategies applicable in a work environment.

That said, individuals with ODD can find rewarding and successful careers when they pursue jobs that cater to their unique strengths and preferences. By considering careers in creative arts, entrepreneurship, problem-solving fields, or physical occupations, people with ODD can flourish in the workforce and create a meaningful and gratifying professional life.

SELF-ANALYSIS QUESTIONNAIRE FOR PARENTS MANAGING A CHILD WITH ODD

1. What is one new system you learned for managing your child's impulsivity or absence of restraint? How might you carry it out at home?
2. Think about a situation where your child lacked empathy toward someone else. How did you manage it? What could you have done differently, considering the situational solutions provided in this section?
3. Contemplate your child's disorganization and difficulty keeping track of belongings. What routines or systems might you create to help them become more organized? How can you use positive reinforcement to encourage this behavior?
4. Recall a recent instance when your child was defensive or easily agitated. How did you respond at the time? What strategies could you use in the future to promote open communication and respectful behavior?
5. Reflect on a recent event where your child exhibited low tolerance for frustration. What coping mechanisms could you teach them to manage frustration, such as taking breaks or encouraging positive self-talk?

1. Examine your child's defiance. How can you provide clear instructions and use positive language to encourage proper behavior? What positive reinforcement techniques could you use to reward appropriate conduct?
2. Consider a situation where your child employed manipulative tactics to get what they wanted. How can you establish clear expectations and consequences to discourage this behavior? How can you demonstrate honest and transparent behavior?

INTERACTIVE ELEMENT

Here is a template for a behavioral contract for your child:

Behavior Contract

Child's Name:

Behavior/Task (specific behavior or task that needs improvement):

_____

_____

_____

Practical Examples: Here are examples of what the behavior/task looks like, such as "raising hand before speaking," "keeping a calm tone when speaking to an elder," or "listening when spoken to."

Consequence/Reward (consequence or reward for achieving or not achieving the behavior/task):

_____

_____

_____

_____

_____

_____

Task or Behavior Measurement:

- Mon
- Tue
- Wed
- Thu
- Fri
- Sat
- Sun

I, _____, agree to work toward achieving the behavior or task outlined in this contract. I understand that by doing so, I will receive the consequence or reward outlined above. I also understand that my progress will be monitored and measured as this contract outlines.

Child's Signature:

_____

Date:

_____

Parent's Signature:

_____

Date:

STORY

Throughout the pages of this book, we have witnessed Ethan's emotional journey. It serves as evidence that regardless of the severity of a child's behavioral challenges, they can receive assistance with affection and appropriate medical care.

Regrettably, many individuals still approach such issues in a manner that only worsens the problem. They might impose various forms of punishment on the child or completely give up, leaving them at the mercy of the disorder. Since you are currently engaged with this book, it can be inferred that, like Theresa in the story, you are receptive to tried-and-tested solutions and are actively seeking methods to help your child triumph over ODD.

Within these pages, I have integrated interactive elements and reflection sections at the end of each chapter, providing a comprehensive approach to consolidate your insights and chart your course forward. My knowledge informs the inclusion of essential medical clarifications and trigger alerts when necessary. For a broader perspective, consider exploring my other impactful works, including "Defusing Explosive Behavior," "Parenting a Child with ADHD," and

"Special Education Playbook for Parents." I invite you to connect with me on Amazon to stay updated on my latest publications and offerings.

One supportive asset for families managing this disorder is the website Empowering Parents, which gives guidance and systems for parenting children with behavioral disorders.

In an article on another website, Comprehensive Youth Services, consultants Kim Abraham and Marney Studaker-Cordner share their encounters bringing up children with ODD and give tips for making outcomes work (Abraham & Studaker-Cordner, 2012). They recommend setting clear expectations and outcomes, using positive reinforcement to empower positive behavior, and looking for outside support from specialists or support groups.

CONCLUSION

The more you learn about the nature of defiance in children, the less you will view it as "something wrong with your child," the more you will see it as a difficult situation or pattern of interactions with highly workable solutions.

— RUSSELL A. BARKLEY

What are the signs, symptoms, and basic need-to-know facts about ODD? Chapter 1 acquainted us with ODD's signs, symptoms, and fundamental realities. It examined the different symptoms that might introduce themselves, like successive fits, extreme contending with grown-ups, dynamic rebellion, and refusal to consent to rules, and it gave an outline of what ODD is and what it means for children.

The second chapter explored various contributing elements that might give rise to ODD. The conversation highlighted the relationship among genetic, environmental, and social factors in determining the development of this condition.

Chapter 3 addressed the misguided judgments and shame encompassing ODD and how they can cause disarray for parents and guardians. It explained that ODD is, much of the time, misunderstood and that many individuals accept it as a consequence of poor parenting or terrible behavior when, truth is told, a genuine disorder requires legitimate treatment and support.

Chapter 4 discussed the possibility that while ODD can be challenging to manage, it can lead to a surprisingly good turn of events. It examined how ODD can assist children with creating important fundamental abilities like freedom, strength, and decisiveness. It gave tips on how parents can work with their child to transform the disorder into a positive encounter.

Chapter 5 presented a 7-step approach to aid parents and caregivers in managing ODD and creating a better experience for everyone involved. The chapter emphasized the significance of establishing clear boundaries and expectations, applying positive reinforcement, maintaining consistency in discipline, and providing practical advice for implementing each step.

Chapter 6 focused on reducing triggers and stress points to enhance the home environment for everyone. This chapter explained how fostering a safe and supportive atmosphere can help children with ODD feel more secure and less prone to outbursts, offering suggestions for minimizing triggers and cultivating a positive home setting.

Chapter 7 provided insights into various conventional and alternative treatment avenues for parents and caregivers when dealing with ODD. It underscored the significance of conventional approaches such as medication and therapy while shedding light on the efficacy of alternative strategies like dietary modifications, physical activity, and natural remedies in symptom management.

Lastly, Chapter 8 provided an overview of common challenges faced by parents dealing with ODD and shared practical guidance on tackling each issue. It covered topics such as communication breakdowns, school-related concerns, and handling difficult behavior in public, offering tips and techniques for addressing each situation.

Parenting a child with ODD can be incredibly challenging, but it is important to start each day anew and do your best in it. More than half the struggle is already overcome by being prepared and knowledgeable.

Let us refer to the heartwarming story from ADDitude Magazine about a mother discovering that her child's oppositional and defiant behavior was a symptom of ODD and ADHD. The child's behavior steadily progressed with a mix of therapeutic approaches, appropriate medications, and refined parenting skills, resulting in a more harmonious family dynamic (Frye, 2022). This inspiring account underscores the importance of having the proper guidance and resources, which can enable the successful handling of ODD while fostering a supportive atmosphere for the child and family alike.

As you progress, consider detailing the next steps to address your child's ODD. Ask yourself the following questions:

- What treatment options will you explore for your child?
- How can you create a safe and supportive environment at home?
- What strategies will you implement to improve communication and manage difficult behavior?
- How can you prioritize your well-being while ensuring you are not overly critical of yourself?

By addressing these considerations and devising a strategy, you will be better prepared to tackle the hurdles of raising a child with ODD.

Remember that you have a support system, and assistance is available to help you and your child traverse this path as a team. Remain steadfast and adopt an optimistic attitude, realizing that with perseverance, empathy, and resolve, you have the power to guide your child past the challenges linked to ODD, ultimately helping them lead a gratifying life.

A Shining Opportunity To Help Another Parent

WANT TO HELP OTHERS?

You've embarked on an incredible journey, and your dedication to understanding and helping your child with Oppositional Defiant Disorder (ODD) is truly commendable. Everything you've absorbed from "Defusing Oppositional Defiant Disorder" is a valuable tool on your path, and now you can extend that help to other parents.

Sharing your honest Amazon review will guide other parents to this resource, offering insights and strategies. Whether time-constrained or not, your review can be a beacon for those seeking ODD support. Consider leaving a video review highlighting your favorite parts for added impact, helping parents discover this invaluable resource.

Your support is not only appreciated but essential. In these transformative times, extending a helping hand to fellow parents equips us all to build a strong and understanding community. Thank you for your dedication and for considering sharing your review, whether written or in video format, to empower others on their ODD journey.

Scan the QR codes to leave a review!

In the United States

In the United Kingdom

REFERENCES

Abraham, K. & Studaker-Cordner, M. (2012, May 5). *Defiant child behavior.* Comprehensive Youth Services of Fresno. https://cysfresno.org/defiant-child-behavior-is-your-children-bad-behavior-escalating/

ADDitude Editors. (2022, April 14). *Play therapy techniques and games to try at home.* ADDitude. https://www.additudemag.com/fun-games-help-adhd-children-learn-from-play/

ADDitude Editors. (2022, November 18). *What is an IEP? Everything you need to know about IDEA, IEPs, and 504 plans.* ADDitude. https://www.google.com/amp/s/www.additudemag.com/iep-vs-504-plan-idea-adhd-disability-education/amp/

Alexa, M. (2014, December 26). *Oppositional defiant disorder treatment - An ODD case study.* Autism 360TM. https://www.autism360.com/opposi tional-defiant-disorder-treatment-and-odd-case-study/

Althoff, R., Kuny-Slock, A., Verhulst, F., Hudziak, J., & Ende, J. van der. (2014). *Classes of oppositional-defiant behavior: Concurrent and predictive validity.* Journal of Child Psychology and Psychiatry, and Allied Disciplines. https://www.semanticscholar.org/paper/Classes-of-oppositional-defiant-behavior%3A-and-Althoff-Kuny-Slock/75db24f5157561653162c5769877d307dc065294

Amen, G. D. (n.d.). *Oppositional defiant disorder.* Amen Clinics. https://www.amenclinics.com/conditions/oppositional-defiant-disorder/#:~:text=ODD%20Brains%20Work%20Differently,one%20activity%20to%20the%20next.

Angoff, L. (n.d.). *Explaining (reframing) oppositional behavior to children.* Brain Building Book. https://brainbuildingbook.com/explaining-behavior/

Asherson, P., Young, A. H., Eich-Höchli, D., Moran, P., Porsdal, V., & Deberdt, W. (2014). Differential diagnosis, comorbidity, and treatment of attention-deficit/hyperactivity disorder in relation to bipolar disorder or borderline personality disorder in adults. *Current Medical Research and Opinion, 30(8),* 1657–1672. https://doi.org/10.1185/03007995.2014.915800

Audio Meditations. (n.d.). HelpGuide. https://www.helpguide.org/home-pages/audio-meditations.htm

Behavior or conduct problems. (2023, March 8). Centers for Disease Control and Prevention. https://www.cdc.gov/childrensmentalhealth/behavior.html

Bernstein, P. S., Ahmed, F., Liu, A., Allman, S., Sheng, X., Sharifzadeh, M., Ermakov, I., & Gellermann, W. (2012). Macular pigment imaging in AREDS2 participants: An ancillary study of AREDS2 subjects enrolled at the Moran Eye Center. *Investigative Ophthalmology & Visual Science, 53(10)*, 6178. https://doi.org/10.1167/iovs.12-10275

Blair, J. R. (2016). The Neurobiology of disruptive behavior disorder. *American Journal of Psychiatry, 173(11)*, 1073–1074. https://doi.org/10.1176/appi.ajp.2016.16080971

Blair, R. J. R. (2013). The neurobiology of psychopathic traits in youths. *Nature Reviews Neuroscience, 14(11)*, 786–799. https://doi.org/10.1038/nrn3577

Bowler, A. (2018, January 26). *Dear parents of children with oppositional defiant behaviour: it is not just you.* Creative Connected Parenting. https://ameliabehaviour.com/harsh-avoidant-parenting-patterns/

Bowler A. (2018, March 1). *Staying on track: Successful communication with your defiant child.* Creative Connected Parenting. https://ameliabehaviour.com/successful-communication-defiant-child/

Burke, J. D., Loeber, R., & Birmaher, B. (2002). Oppositional defiant disorder and conduct disorder: A review of the past 10 years, part II. *Journal of the American Academy of Child & Adolescent Psychiatry, 41(11)*, 1275–1293. https://doi.org/10.1097/00004583-200211000-00009

Burke, J. D., Waldman, I., & Lahey, B. B. (2010). Predictive validity of childhood oppositional defiant disorder and conduct disorder: Implications for the DSM-V. *Journal of Abnormal Psychology, 119(4)*, 739–751. https://doi.org/10.1037/a0019708

Calub, C. A., Rapport, M. D., & Alexander, K. (2020, September 13). Reducing aggression using a multimodal cognitive behavioral treatment approach: A case study of a preschooler with oppositional defiant disorder. *Sage Journals, 20(1)*. https://doi.org/10.1177/1534650120958069

Canino, G., Polanczyk, G., Bauermeister, J. J., Rohde, L. A., & Frick, P. J. (2010, June 9). Does the prevalence of CD and ODD vary across cultures? *Social*

Psychiatry and Psychiatric Epidemiology, 45(7), 695–704. https://doi.org/10.1007/s00127-010-0242-y

Connor, D. (2002, February). Preschool attention deficit hyperactivity disorder: A review of prevalence, diagnosis, neurobiology, and stimulant treatment. *Journal of Developmental and Behavioral Pediatrics, 23(0)*, S1-S9. https://journals.lww.com/jrnldbp/Fulltext/2002/02001/Preschool_Attention_Deficit_Hyperactivity.2.aspx

Connor, D. F., & Doerfler, L. A. (2008, September). ADHD with comorbid oppositional defiant disorder or conduct disorder. *Journal of Attention Disorders, 12(2)*, 126–134. https://doi.org/10.1177/1087054707308486

Corcoran, J. (2003, March). Behavioral parent training with oppositional defiant disorder. *Oxford Academic*, 36-55. https://doi.org/10.1093/acprof:oso/9780195149524.003.0002

Cortese, S., Holtmann, M., Banaschewski, T., Buitelaar, J., Coghill, D., Danckaerts, M., Dittmann, R. W., Graham, J., Taylor, E., & Sergeant, J. (2013, January 7). Practitioner Review: Current best practice in the management of adverse events during treatment with ADHD medications in children and adolescents. *Journal of Child Psychology and Psychiatry, 54(3)*, 227–246. https://doi.org/10.1111/jcpp.12036

Cunningham, C. E., McHolm, A., Boyle, M. H., & Patel, S. (2008). Behavioral and emotional adjustment, family functioning, academic performance, and social relationships in children with selective mutism. *Journal of Child Psychology and Psychiatry, and Allied Disciplines, 45(8)*, 1363–1372. https://doi.org/10.1111/j.1469-7610.2004.00843.x

David Maraniss quotes. (n.d.). Brainy Quote. https://www.brainyquote.com/authors/david-maraniss-quotes#:~:text=I%20believe%20that%20life%20is,its%20endless%20mystery%20and%20wonder.

Diagnostic and statistical manual of mental disorders: DSM-5TM, 5th ed. (2013). Psycnet.apa.org. https://dsm.psychiatryonline.org/doi/book/10.1176/appi.books.9780890425596

Dietzman, A. (n.d.). *5 ways to help k–12 students advocate for themselves.* Tutor.com. https://www.tutor.com/articles/5-ways-to-help-k-12-students-advocate-for-themselves

Dieken, C. (2005). *Oppositional defiant disorder: Using family therapy and parent training techniques for effective treatment outcomes training techniques for effec-*

tive treatment outcomes. University of Northern Iowa. https://scholarworks.
uni.edu/cgi/viewcontent.cgi?article=1538&context=grp

DSM-5 child mental disorder classification. (n.d.). Substance Abuse and Mental
Health Services Administration. https://www.ncbi.nlm.nih.gov/
books/NBK519712/?report=reader#_NBK519712_pubdet_

Ehmke, R. (2017, October 12). *What is oppositional defiant disorder?* Child Mind
Institute. https://childmind.org/article/what-is-odd-oppositional-defi
ant-disorder/

Eyberg, S. M., Nelson, M. M., & Boggs, S. R. (2008, April 15). Evidence-based
psychosocial treatments for children and adolescents with disruptive
behavior. *Journal of Clinical Child & Adolescent Psychology, 37(1),* 215–237.
https://doi.org/10.1080/15374410701820117

Faraone, S. V., & Larsson, H. (2019). Genetics of attention deficit hyperactivity disorder. *Molecular Psychiatry, 24,* 562–575. https://www.nature.
com/articles/s41380-018-0070-0

Frequently asked questions. (n.d.). American Academy of Child and Adolescent
Psychology. https://www.aacap.org/
aacap/Families_and_Youth/Resource_Centers/Oppositional_Defiant_Dis
order_Resource_Center/FAQ.aspx#:~:text=Oppositional%20Defiant%
20Disorder%20(ODD)%20is

Frye, D. (2022, March 31). *Back from the brink: Two families' stories of oppositional defiant disorder.* ADDitude. https://www.additudemag.com/opposi
tional-defiant-disorder-adhd-family-stories/

Furnham, A, & Lousley, C. (2013, March 29). Mental health literacy and the
anxiety disorders. *Health, 5(3).* https://www.scirp.org/(S(351jmbntvn
sjt1aadkposzje))/reference/referencespapers.aspx?referenceid=765573

Genetics play a significant role in immunity. (2017, January 5). ScienceDaily.
https://www.sciencedaily.com/releases/2017/01/170105082755.htm

Ghosh, A., Ray, A., & Basu, A. (2017, November 29). Oppositional defiant
disorder: Current insight. *Psychology Research and Behavior Management, 10,*
353–367. https://doi.org/10.2147/prbm.s120582

Harada, Y., Saitoh, K., Iida, J., Sakuma, A., Iwasaka, H., Imai, J., Hirabayashi,
M., Yamada, S., Hirabayashi, S., Uchiyama, T., Ohta, S., & Amano, N.
(2004, June 1). *The reliability and validity of the oppositional defiant behavior
inventory.* European Child & Adolescent Psychiatry. https://www.semantic

scholar.org/paper/The-reliability-and-validity-of-the-Oppositional-Harada-Saitoh/13195890a4da27468e646848185a4d910eef77a5

Health Match staff (2022, May 10). *Can you take magnesium for anxiety?*. Health Match. https://healthmatch.io/anxiety/can-you-take-magnesium-for-anxiety#what-kind-of-magnesium-should-i-take

Herrity, J. (2022, October 1). *Guide on how to write smart goals (with examples)*. Indeed. https://www.indeed.com/career-advice/career-development/how-to-write-smart-goals

How do I choose between medication and therapy?. (2017, July). American Psychological Association. https://www.apa.org/ptsd-guideline/patients-and-families/medication-or-therapy

How much sleep children need. (2022, September 16). Cleveland Clinic. https://health.clevelandclinic.org/recommended-amount-of-sleep-for-children/

"If you want something you have never had, you must be willing to do something you have never done." (n.d.). Quotefancy. https://quotefancy.com/quote/168888/Thomas-Jefferson-If-you-want-something-you-have-never-had-you-must-be-willing-to-do

Jackee Harry quotes. (n.d.). Brainy Quote. https://www.brainyquote.com/quotes/jackee_harry_490008

Keohane, C. E., Steele, A. D., Fetzer, C., Khowsathit, J., Tyne, D. V., Moynié, L., Gilmore, M. S., Karanicolas, J., Sieber, S. A., & Wuest, W. M. (2018). Promysalin elicits species-selective inhibition of pseudomonas aeruginosa by targeting succinate dehydrogenase. *Journal of the American Chemical Society, 140*(5), 1774–1782. https://doi.org/10.1021/jacs.7b11212

Kyeva, B. L., Ireri, W. N., & Menecha, B. J. (2021, Aug 5). The prevalence of oppositional defiant disorder and its impact on the academic performance of secondary school students: A case of selected public schools in Kibwezi Sub-County, Makueni County, Kenya. *Journal of Sociology, Psychology & Religious Studies, 2*(3), 91-99. https://stratfordjournals.org/journals/index.php/Journal-of-Sociology-Psychology/article/view/853

Lee, K. (2020, May 3). *Effective ways to handle defiant children*. VeryWell Family. https://www.verywellfamily.com/how-to-handle-defiant-children-620106

Lee, P., Lee, T., Chen, V. C., Chen, M., Shih, D., Shao, W., & Lee, M. (2010, June). Quality of life in mothers of children with oppositional defiant symptoms: a community sample. *Mental Health in Family Medicine, 7(2),* 93–100. https://www.ncbi.nlm.nih.gov/pmc/articles/PMC2939462/

Lehman, J. (n.d.). *Oppositional defiant children: Why "no" sets them off.* Empowering Parents. https://www.empoweringparents.com/article/why-the-word-no-sets-off-an-oppositional-defiant-child/

Lehman, J. (2011, June 20). *4 ways to manage oppositional defiant disorder in children.* Psych Central. https://psychcentral.com/blog/4-ways-to-manage-oppositional-defiant-disorder-in-children#1

Levings, K. (2020, April 13). *7 effective communication techniques to manage defiant students.* Insights to Behavior. https://insightstobehavior.com/blog/7-effective-communication-techniques-manage-defiant-students/

Lindberg, S. & Weiss, K. (2023, March 21). *22 ways to calm yourself down.* Healthline. https://www.healthline.com/health/how-to-calm-down

Logsdon, A. (2020, July 24). *What is oppositional defiant disorder (ODD)?* VeryWell Mind. https://www.verywellmind.com/what-is-oppositional-defiant-disorder-2161913

Loop, E. (2017, June 13). *Activities for oppositional defiant children.* Healthfully. https://healthfully.com/1006434-activities-oppositional-defiant-children.html

Marsh, A. A., Finger, E. C., Mitchell, D. G. V., Reid, M. E., Sims, C., Kosson, D. S., Towbin, K. E., Leibenluft, E., Pine, D. S., & Blair, R. J. R. (2008). Reduced amygdala response to fearful expressions in children and adolescents with callous-unemotional traits and disruptive behavior disorders. *American Journal of Psychiatry, 165(6),* 712–720. https://doi.org/10.1176/appi.ajp.2007.07071145

Matthys, W., Vanderschuren, L. J. M. J., & Schutter, D. J. L. G. (2012). The neurobiology of oppositional defiant disorder and conduct disorder: Altered functioning in three mental domains. *Development and Psychopathology, 25(1),* 193–207. https://doi.org/10.1017/s0954579412000272

Memon, N. (n.d.). *What are typical behaviors of a child?.* MedicineNet. https://www.medicinenet.com/what_are_typical_behaviors_of_a_child/article.htm

Miller, E. K., & Cohen, J. D. (2001). An integrative theory of prefrontal cortex function. *Annual Review of Neuroscience, 24(1),* 167–202. https://doi.org/10.1146/annurev.neuro.24.1.167

Mitchison, G. M., Liber, J. M., Hannesdottir, D. K., & Njardvik, U. (2020, February). Emotion dysregulation, ODD and conduct problems in a sample of five and six-year-old children. *Child psychiatry and human development, 51(1)*, 71–79. https://doi.org/10.1007/s10578-019-00911-7

Moffitt, T. E., Arseneault, L., Jaffee, S. R., Kim-Cohen, J., Koenen, K. C., Odgers, C. L., Slutske, W. S., & Viding, E. (2008, January). Research Review: DSM-V conduct disorder: research needs for an evidence base. *Journal of Child Psychology and Psychiatry, 49(1)*, 3–33. https://doi.org/10.1111/j.1469-7610.2007.01823.x

Motivational Quotes. (n.d.). Quotefancy. https://quotefancy.com/motivational-quotes

Neil deGrasse Tyson quotes. (n.d.). Brainy Quote. https://www.brainyquote.com/quotes/neil_degrasse_tyson_531089

Nock, M. K., Kazdin, A. E., Hiripi, E., & Kessler, R. C. (2006). Prevalence, subtypes, and correlates of DSM-IV conduct disorder in the National Comorbidity Survey Replication. *Psychological Medicine, 36(5)*, 699. https://doi.org/10.1017/s0033291706007082

Nock, M., & Kazdin, A. (2001, June). Parent expectancies for child therapy: assessment and relation to participation in treatment. *Journal of Child and Family Studies, 10(2)*, 155–180. https://projects.iq.harvard.edu/files/nocklab/files/nock_2001_parentexpectancies_childtherapy_jcfs.pdf

Noordermeer, S. D. S., Luman, M., & Oosterlaan, J. (2016, March). A systematic review and meta-analysis of neuroimaging in Oppositional Defiant Disorder (ODD) and Conduct Disorder (CD) taking Attention-Deficit Hyperactivity Disorder (ADHD) into account. *Neuropsychology Review, 26*, 44-72. https://doi.org/10.1007%2Fs11065-015-9315-8

Oppositional/defiant disorder ages 6-12. (2018, November 24). The Whole Child. https://www.thewholechild.org/parent-resources/age-6-12/oppositional-defiant-disorder-ages-6-12/

Oppositional defiant disorder (ODD). (2023, January 4). Mayo Clinic. https://www.mayoclinic.org/diseases-conditions/oppositional-defiant-disorder/symptoms-causes/syc-20375831

Oppositional defiant disorder (ODD). (2022, May 16). Cleveland Clinic. https://my.clevelandclinic.org/health/diseases/9905-oppositional-defiant-disorder

Oppositional defiant disorder. (2022, November 28). WebMD. https://www.webmd.com/mental-health/oppositional-defiant-disorder

Oppositional defiant disorder. (n.d.). Newport Academy. https://www.newportacademy.com/resources/glossary/oppositional-defiant-disorder/#:~:text=What%20Is%20Oppositional%20Defiant%20Disorder

Oppositional defiant disorder (ODD): Children and pre-teens. (2022, December 31). Raising Children Network. https://raisingchildren.net.au/school-age/health-daily-care/school-age-mental-health-concerns/odd

Oppositional Defiant Disorder (ODD). (2022, May 16). Cleveland Clinic. https://my.clevelandclinic.org/health/diseases/9905-oppositional-defiant-disorder#

Oruche, U. M., Draucker, C., Alkhattab, H., Knopf, A., & Mazurcyk, J. (2014, August). Interventions for family members of adolescents with disruptive behavior disorders. *Journal of Child and Adolescent Psychiatric Nursing, 27(3),* 99–108. https://doi.org/10.1111/jcap.12078

Pierce, L. (2020, September 26). *OCD, self injury, and suicidal thoughts.* Verywell Mind. https://www.verywellmind.com/ocd-self-injury-and-suicidal-thoughts-2510599

Papadopoulos, L. (2018, July 17). *Omega-3 supplements may curb disruptive and abusive behavior in children.* Interesting Engineering. https://interestingengineering.com/science/omega-3-supplements-may-curb-disruptive-and-abusive-behavior-in-children

Posner, J., Kass, E., & Hulvershorn, L. (2014). Using Stimulants to Treat ADHD-related emotional lability. *Current Psychiatry Reports, 16(10).* https://doi.org/10.1007/s11920-014-0478-4

Quick guide to oppositional defiant disorder. (2023, February 23). Child Mind Institute. https://childmind.org/guide/quick-guide-to-oppositional-defiant-disorder/

Ralph Marston quotes. (n.d.). Brainy Quote. https://www.brainyquote.com/quotes/ralph_marston_132916

Ramamani Iyengar memorial yoga institute. (n.d.). Google Arts & Culture. https://artsandculture.google.com/story/yoga-for-mind-and-body-ramamani-iyengar-memorial-yoga-institute/0QXRdphJ0xcG8Q?hl=en

Raypole, C. & Gotter, A. (2021, December 3). *Understanding oppositional defiant disorder.* Healthline. https://www.healthline.com/health/oppositional-defiant-disorder

Reid, S. (n.d.). *Autism treatments, therapies, and interventions*. HelpGuide. https://www.helpguide.org/articles/autism-learning-disabilities/autism-treatments-therapies-interventions.htm

Robinson, L. & Segal, J. (n.d.). *Help for parents of troubled teens*. HelpGuide. https://www.helpguide.org/articles/parenting-family/helping-troubled-teens.htm

Rubia, K. (2010). "Cool" inferior frontostriatal dysfunction in attention-deficit/hyperactivity disorder versus "hot" ventromedial orbitofrontal-limbic dysfunction in conduct disorder: A review. *Biological Psychiatry, 69*(12), e69–e87. https://doi.org/10.1016/j.biopsych.2010.09.023

Russell A. Barkley quotes. (n.d.). GoodReads. https://www.goodreads.com/author/quotes/215511.Russell_A_Barkley

75 easy and fun calm down strategies for children. (2022, November 17). Parents with Confidence. https://parentswithconfidence.com/calm-down-strategies-for-children/

Smith, T. (2001). Discrete trial training in the treatment of autism. *Focus on Autism and Other Developmental Disabilities, 16*(2), 86–92. https://doi.org/10.1177/108835760101600204

Sonuga-Barke, E. J. S., Brandeis, D., Cortese, S., Daley, D., Ferrin, M., Holtmann, M., Stevenson, J., Danckaerts, M., van der Oord, S., Döpfner, M., Dittmann, R. W., Simonoff, E., Zuddas, A., Banaschewski, T., Buitelaar, J., Coghill, D., Hollis, C., Konofal, E., Lecendreux, M., & Wong, I. C. K. (2013). Nonpharmacological interventions for adhd: systematic review and meta-analyses of randomized controlled trials of dietary and psychological treatments. *American Journal of Psychiatry, 170*(3), 275–289. https://doi.org/10.1176/appi.ajp.2012.12070991

Stringaris, A., & Goodman, R. (2009). Longitudinal outcome of youth oppositionality: irritable, headstrong, and hurtful behaviors have distinctive predictions. *Journal of the American Academy of Child & Adolescent Psychiatry, 48*(4), 404–412. https://doi.org/10.1097/chi.0b013e3181984f30

Strøm, V., Fønhus, M. S., Ekeland, E., & Jamtvedt, G. (2017). *Physical exercise for oppositional defiant disorder and conduct disorder in children and adolescents*. Cochrane Database of Systematic Reviews. https://doi.org/10.1002/14651858.cd010670.pub2

Thapar, A., Cooper, M., Jefferies, R., & Stergiakouli, E. (2011). What causes attention deficit hyperactivity disorder?. *Archives of Disease in Childhood,*

97(3), 260–265. https://doi.org/10.1136/archdischild-2011-300482

30 journal prompts for parents. (n.d.). Guided Journals and Memory Books. https://robynliechti.com/blogs/journaling-resources/30-days-of-journal-prompts-for-parents

Thompson, H. (2021, May 31). *Oppositional defiant disorder: When your child isn't just "difficult"*. Today's Parent. https://www.todaysparent.com/family/discipline/oppositional-defiance-disorder-when-your-child-isnt-just-difficult/

Triggers, emotional attacks, & emotional safety techniques. (2015, April 7). Kidpower International. https://www.kidpower.org/library/article/triggers-safety-techniques/

Viktor E. Frankl quotes. (n.d.). Brainy Quote. https://www.brainyquote.com/quotes/viktor_e_frankl_160380

Waldman, D. I. (2022, September 9). *Oppositional defiant disorder: Epidemiology, clinical manifestations, course and diagnosis*. UpToDate. https://www.uptodate.com/contents/oppositional-defiant-disorder-epidemiology-clinical-manifestations-course-and-diagnosis#H4195468159

Walter Bagehot quotes. (n.d.). Brainy Quote. https://www.brainyquote.com/quotes/walter_bagehot_136017

What is children's mental health?. (2023, March 8). Centers for Disease Control and Prevention. https://www.cdc.gov/childrensmentalhealth/basics.html#:~:text=Without%20early%20diagnosis%20and%20treatment,that%20can%20continue%20into%20adulthood

Wilson, J. D. (2019, February 27). *Biological, genetic and environmental causes of oppositional defiant disorder*. News Medical & Life Sciences. https://www.google.com/amp/s/www.news-medical.net/amp/health/Biological-Genetic-and-Environmental-Causes-of-Oppositional-Defiant-Disorder.aspx

Your duties and rights as a parent. (2020, September 22). Family & Community Services. https://www.facs.nsw.gov.au/families/parenting/responsibility-and-rights/parent-duties#

Made in the USA
Columbia, SC
08 December 2023

28100540R00112